Bipolar Sagacity Volume 7

(Integrity versus Faithlessness)

Those Sayings, Ruminations, Lamentations, Exhortations, Aphorisms and Questions in Reference to the Spiritual, Physical, Social, Psychological and Vocational Issues of Life

Thomas D. Sharts M.Ed

To order additional copies of this book, contact:
Xlibris
1-888-795-4274
www.Xlibris.com
Orders@Xlibris.com
778358

Bipolar Sagacity Volume 7

(Integrity versus Faithlessness)

Those Sayings, Ruminations, Lamentations, Exhortations, Aphorisms and Questions in Reference to the Spiritual, Physical, Social, Psychological and Vocational Issues of Life

Thomas D. Sharts M.Ed

Fantasy is idolatry. TS 18

The curse of humanity is we cannot truly feel other people's pain and that is why humanity will never truly evolve any substantial global social and cultural gain. TS 18

Your unwillingness to change is really behind your chronic depression and failure; yet, that fact might not be readily apparent to your conscious mind. TS 18

And how many people are terrible persons and they don't even really know it because they have never exercised any contemplation to make that necessary discovery? TS 18

Redundancy is a bore. TS 18

And where is the math more unforgiving assuming the greatest consequence but in the example of driving on the road where you might get it right 999,999 thousand times and the one time you don't get it right (because you're turning your head to look at the beautiful girl that lasts beyond one second) you're now dead. TS 18

And think of how many people will never be asking you out for a cup of coffee? TS 18

A primary explanation for obesity is inverted sexual energy. TS 18

The sham life is the corporate business suit and tie that never achieves anything while wearing the suit and tie. TS 18

If you doubt the love of Almighty God, then lay eyes upon the beautiful little girl in front of you. TS 18

The management team that's always saying *"no"* really blows and they'll never be in the know because they blow! TS 18

When all that's left in your life is to be pure, now you're on the cusp of your cure. TS 18

The pure vessel of love is your hope – not smoking dope. TS 18

Move beyond living in between and become clean and realize the highest esteem. TS 18

The joy of Trini is she is no meanie. TS 18

Embrace the new day that's come today in order to find a better way and then hear no more nays. TS 18

The purity of a child will keep you from going wild lest you become overwhelmingly defiled. TS 18

Don't live like a corrupt King who has many illicit flings because then you'll never joyfully sing. TS 18

The idolatrous western church is dead so how can anyone be led and fed? TS 18

Vionye is like the beauty of a blue sky and I hope her smiling grace never dies. TS 18

And how many young fellas want McKaella? TS 18

Get-off your smartphone and be known in the real-life zone. TS 18

The called leader is in another spiritual place that unfortunately, leaves him as a socially-isolated head case. TS 18

Don't be a social clown that's widely known around town, instead do something with your life that will utterly astound! TS 18

If there's anything certainly for sure, now is the time to become fully spiritually, physically, psychologically and socially pure. TS 18

Dead in the water in your sins means you need Almighty God to send you some life-saving fins. TS 18

The irony and beauty of isolation is that is where purity can be found. TS 18

What do you think you know until it has been a year since you have been able to painlessly bite into a roll? TS 18

Pray for Jesus to come before you die as a forsaken bum. TS 18

The man who is a habitual sinner can never become a consistent winner. TS 18

Unfortunately, getting drunk cannot get you out of your perennial funk nor can becoming a monk, and likewise, either way you're sunk! TS 18

The redundant academician is a bore. TS 18

When the girls are on the lag and the guys line-up at the bar going stag, you know none of these dudes have it in the bag and some have even turned into fags rather than get a bottom-of-the barrel hag, yet that's far better than dressing-up in drag. TS 18

The needy souls surround and the personal salvation needs of those multitudes abounds. TS 18

If the Holy Spirit has evolved mercy and compassion in you, now you join the few who actually have a clue of what to do in order to get this world out of the loo. TS 18

Evoke the purity of the motive of what you desire and maybe that request will not burn-up in the judgment of fire. TS 18

Have a little confidence and maybe that will be the difference of her saying "yes" rather than "no!" TS 18

If you know he's hiding something, then it's likely he's hiding something. TS 18

As long as humans exist, then stress will always be a factor as a significant independent variable in play. TS 18

The too time-managed and organized man makes the serendipitous happening an impossibility and he loses some beautiful blessings because of it. TS 18

The collective global world has taken a shit and henceforth because of it, many people are having fits or blowing their brains out to bits as ignorant nimwits are running aground while governing their ships into the bottomless pit. TS 18

Leave the idolatrous material world behind that's always placing people in an economic bind and discover that there's life for people who aren't greedy and blind. TS 18

The hell-bent pursuit of false intimacy will make a man into another man that's fit for the can. TS 18

The deprived in their sins are further punished as their grief remains unending. TS 18

As holy as a man is, the darkness within him still remains like a dormant volcano. TS 18

The wise man is always prepared for the worst, yet he knows that Almighty Lord God is his trust and strength. TS 18

When the sinning remains unabated in its hell-bent drive, then the wellspring of knowledge just trickles out like the weak piss stream of an old man. TS 18

Inspiration is the artist's creative tool, but his hell-bent sins reduce him to a lame fool because his mind has devolved into a diabolical cesspool. TS 18

Find your confessional booth to tell the truth about the condition of your lying soul before your life suffers a tragic toll. TS 18

The man's life that completely sucks is more than likely stuck in some socioeconomic muck that is running his life amok, yet no one will help him, but they will gleefully tell him, "Rotsa Ruck!" TS 18

The Son of Man had no place to lay his head (and maybe you likewise) because the world is spiritually dead. TS 18

The potter's wheel shaping your divine purity to become a reality is: hate, jealousy, injustice, the world's ignorance, cowardice, irrational fear, lust and greed. TS 18

The builder without anything to build is like the ice cream cone without the milk. TS 18

Self-destruction's will is fueled by a lack of love realized. TS 18

In one's life, the time to shine equates to the worth of a dime whereas most of what we do is fritter away time. TS 18

Sometimes, all that's it is you sitting in the shit. TS 18

And what debilitates the heart more than knowing all that should have been realized that never was realized? TS 18

Confess your troubled heart and be smart in order to get a viable new start lest your spirit for realizing meaningful living falls apart. TS 18

I definitely need a maid and some pink lemonade and to get seriously paid lest I steadily fade. TS 18

Monogamy fails because it ends the flirting and the dance of wanting and being wanted. TS 18

The man perennially alone sees his soul get worn down to the bone and he desperately needs to be shown that his life won't take a better attitudinal tone as a result of getting a shitty loan or a new smartphone. TS 18

And the disgrace of humanity is the little babies living in blight and masses of people with wealthy resources to help are not willing to take the babies out of such oppressive environmental sites. TS 18

When your life is utterly boring you definitely won't be soaring but you just might be mourning. TS 18

The man with no rest will soon run-out of zest to be his best and what it will take for him to repent of his hell-bent work-a-holism is anyone's guess. TS 18

Your life out of the starting gate should ultimately evolve with you getting your life straight and henceforth realizing a far better fate. TS18

To apprehend a love of your life closes-out your internal strife. TS 18

Growing a love can be hard work only for the selfish ignorant jerk. TS 18

Some people need to be shown how to change their shitty attitudinal tone, and yet others will refuse such instruction in order to continue to piss and moan. TS 18

The man with hope never forsakes the soap. TS 18

Is the blessing of the cyclical nature of life an indication of Almighty God's love and salvation? TS 18

Superficiality is: having no well-being for your soul. TS 18

Sin can actually become quite the bore. TS 18

So much unsaid is responsible for people being dead – when instead - they could have been spiritually, physically, socially, psychologically and vocationally fed rather than blowing their brains-out in the backyard shed. TS 18

The man without any self-control is in a pretty sorry hole, and more than likely for Christmas, will be getting a box of coal and not some bowl of Honeynut Cheerios as a result of being such a complete zero rather than a Good Joe! TS 18

The vacuum of aimlessness is lust and it will surely suck you up! TS 18

Her late entrance means she's digging you. TS 18

The world of should of and could of, should permanently be gotten rid of. TS 18

And what is the sum of those people chasing elusive orgasms? TS 18

Florita is a beauty at sixty so when she was thirty, her loveliness must have been criminal. TS 18

For some, securing the time to pursue and conquest their lust is their securing trust. TS 18

Lust and purity are a fine line. TS 18

Having powerful virility and humility is a rare combination indeed. TS 18

The physical senses are our *living electric grid* that makes living a vital life possible. Therefore, thank Almighty Father God for this great blessing upon humanity. TS 18

Lord, get us back on the rail before we get a powerful kick in the tail without fail. TS 18

The tragedy of life is so much has already occurred that has flown-away like a wayward bird. TS 18

If you're holding your breath for justice to be realized upon earth, you will be CEM-bound soon. TS 18

Religion: Man's futile attempt to explain an infinite God. TS 18

Sin is kryptonite to the body and soul. TS 18

Your exhaustion knows no bounds and only serves to make you look like a useless clown. TS 18

Burying you passions has a price. TS 18

For everything gained there is a loss whether you're perceptually aware of it or not. TS 18

The consistently reticent man is rarely respected. TS 18

It's amazing how many people cannot offer the sacrifice of their thanksgiving or awareness in order to minister to those people that have a serious fallible need. TS 18

We set in place our own prisons and the boundaries that limit our growth as spiritual, physical, social, psychological and vocational beings. TS 18

Your non-attendance precludes you the opportunities to learn what you need to know in order to be the best beyond the rest. TS 18

Not being inwardly known does not take you toward many pleasant places in this life. TS 18

Our deceived selves have created an opportunity where the majority of us will watch the majority of what we have lived for burn-up in the fire of judgment and the majority of us will receive no reward but the left-over ashes. TS 18

The *no one cares spirit* is pretty dense in some places. TS 18

Mass blank faces in the audience don't inspire the speaker, but rather suck the life out of him. TS 18

The younger generation's refusal to learn from the older generation regarding the issues of life keeps the human race treading water in the sea of limbo. TS 18

So many people already dead and buried that were so-called vital and productive people upon earth; and yet, the majority of living persons don't even know who they were by name. Classic. TS 18

The pursuit of mammon or a particular status is nothing to be proud of. TS 18

Frittering away your time watching TV crime will never get you into that passionate loving 69. TS 18

Sometimes, your sacrificial giving is like hosing down the sidewalk; you can clean it, but you cannot grow it or make it more productive. TS 18

There are people all-around you that need to make decisions that they're not willing to make or will ever make and it's more than likely a huge mistake. TS 18

The person we memorialize doesn't get anything out of it because he/she is on the other side of the universe at that point. TS 18

The man that has lived long-term austerity derives the great blessing of gaining some serious clarity. TS 18

The rightful choice for choosing the appointed leader is identifying the person who has complete self-control for clarity's sake, and henceforth, can make the correct decision every time. TS 18

Living for the moment is going to cost you some money. TS 18

As the disgrace sits and everything takes a shit and in the meanwhile is blown to bits, sane men are having fits. TS 18

The correct decision to make every time relates to the criteria of truth, merit, justice and equity. TS 18

The delaying of tearing-it-up gives you some rest, but the inevitable time will come like death row's arrival time, and then, tearing-it-up will reign in that moment. TS 18

No contemplation means no worthy art worth a damn. TS 18

The sacrifice is necessary, but the humanness brings the mourning as a result of it. TS 18

The market world pisses upon the sanctity of peace and tranquility. TS 18

Some people will never experience spiritual coital bliss. TS 18

The uselessness of mid-life and old age is like burned toast. TS 18

If you don't love her you don't have to apologize. TS 18

The prison life is in many cases self-imposed; and likewise, social chaos will ensue in order to obliterate it; and for some, that is too steep of a price to assume. TS 18

Zero accolades for years on-end and still productive despite this, awaits the final grand entrance along with the resounding crescendo for a job well done! TS 18

Old age can never entirely cleanse itself from boredom because it's part of the curse. TS 18

Lord, help me change my ways so I can see better days where I don't always have to pay or hear constant nays all freaking day. TS 18

Focusing your energy and time upon addictions that are cheap will surely account for why you'll not be getting any viable sleep. TS 18

Ween yourself-off of what's tearing you apart at the physical seams and get clean in order to realize a new healthy esteem or you'll get inevitably creamed and reamed. TS 18

You may blindly and sedulously adore the girl online who's far away living on a distance shore, but when you actually meet her, you might find out she's not your wannabe whore, and is actually quite a massive bore who only cares about you taking her to another store to buy something more! TS 18

Entrenched personal pride is the foundation of slow suicide that shouldn't be tried based upon the evidence of those who have already gone down the same defied slide and have already died. TS 18

Playing church is for brain-dead conforming self-serving morons. TS 18

The huge hole in your heart is the curse upon the human race associated with the fact that as much as we think we know, we only *know in part* making us lifelong retarts. TS 18

And what sucks the life out of you more than nobody wanting what you're selling? TS 18

Forlorn and torn from an addiction to porn is the person that needs to be reborn in order to rid himself from debasing self-scorn. TS 18

If you marry the compulsive money-hungry chick, then you'll always be needing a drink or a competent well-informed shrink. TS 18

The individual that doesn't habitually contemplatively think is on the spiritual and psychological brink and will certainly sink or find himself needing a competent shrink who is no fink or a complete dink. TS 18

The advisor who sits alone and has no advisee's, wishes it wouldn't be so because all he purely desires is to help people see so they don't live like yo-yos. TS 18

The girls who stay away are the ones who always say "nay" and likewise will continue to suffer on with some lonely frustrating days. TS 18

The *I got mine* mentality of idolatry in the USA fed by erroneous Christian doctrine that believes *God is my Santa Claus* keeps social class divisions in a healthy place. TS 18

The choices we make in most cases, are the choices we want to make and therefore, we should own them. TS 18

When the Holy Spirit leaves a man, he's in trouble. TS 18

Lord, pray for all those people who are waiting to hear some bad news. TS 18

As long as you work for someone else, you're a total slave. Therefore, accept it or change it. TS 18

Having courage when you're alone knows no accolades. TS 18

Unwelcome social change ain't like singing *Home on the Range*. TS 18

When Almighty God bequeaths you a blessing and a new reality, then be thankful for it and secure it. TS 18

If you have lost your way entirely, then you're most assuredly ready to become a retiree. TS 18

The older guys can dream all they want, but they ain't getting the pretty debutante even if they have a magic wand. TS 18

When the things that matter to you fly away, then what do you have now? TS 18

Let today be the day that you find your way and from then on, make sure you stay and don't go astray looking for some undeserved payday. TS 18

So many morons striving to be a star, yet they are so far away from meeting and/or surpassing the qualified bar; and likewise, they'll never be getting that shiny new car. TS 18

One doesn't make millions of dollars being a purely good person. Don't be deceived. TS 18

The incompetent people are the ones who waste their time with behavioral frivolities because that's all they're capable of doing; yet, deceivingly so, they define these futile behavioral exercises as meaningful work. TS 18

Your pretty front lawn cannot save you when your hope is utterly gone. TS 18

The dregs of souls that surround you can truly offer you nothing today and will likewise be doing the same tomorrow regardless of what good news they have been socialized with. TS 18

Suffering in isolation and silence is sorely intense and ultimately makes little sense with no recompense. TS 18

Poverty takes away peoples life goals and puts their souls down the toilet bowl. TS 18

Better to be deceived or blinded by your ignorance to do something with your life rather than doing nothing. TS 18

The man on illicit drugs usually has a sorry looking mug and needs some serious hugs. TS 18

UPS: The tightest ship in the anal business. TS 18

You don't amass a 36 billion dollar personal fortune the honest way. Don't be deceived. TS 18

And you have these billionaires bragging-on their philanthropic endeavors when the real issue is: how much of that capital do they have in their bank accounts as a result of them being an asshole? TS 18

All that work and all that struggling and you're going to die anyway. Hilarious waste of time and purely the epitome of zero logic. TS 18

It's all vanity, and if you're going to apprehend sanity, then reject the insanity that goes with the lifestyle of ignorant vanity. TS 18

Having nothing to do and nowhere to go all of the time is the harbinger of the train wreck to come in your life. TS 18

Death: The ultimate status killer. TS 18

Doing good is a lot like wood; a lot of diverse good will derive from it. TS 18

The life of *everything never being risked in order to stay the same* is quite the shame and will never make it to the wall of fame. TS 18

The cost of death for the wealthy is extraordinarily high. TS 18

You many know a person who's wicked and his/her lying face needs a serious dose of mace. TS 18

So many people find addictions to cope with the daily grind and to unwind when the reality is: such self-destructive choices must be left behind lest they coagulate into a strangling bind. TS 18

Those who are sorely bored might be contemplating a fall upon their sword, yet in actuality, in order to procure meaningful healing, they need to find the Lord. TS 18

What can be done about a wayward son who is having too much fun and has wasted a ton but for him to be won by the Holy Son? TS 18

Finally put away your wayward ways and find a new day where living right may place you in a secure psychological bay with joyful pay. TS 18

You can be so chronically overtired and wired that it could lead to you being fired. TS 18

The power of your willful mind can place you in an entangling bind that ain't so kind and you'll have a difficult time trying to unwind. TS 18

The man in perennial self-doubt is at-risk for becoming chronically strung-out, yet that dysfunctional lifestyle will never help him eradicate his self-doubt without a doubt. TS 18

Not living holy will take its spiritual, physical, psychological, social and vocational tolly. TS 17

Some people add nothing into your life-evolving equation but spiritual energy drainage. TS 18

Some men love to blow as homos, but who knows, maybe there's a chick for them that is yet not known? TS 18

The man who collects wealth defies himself. TS 18

The man with nothing left will not evolve his skill set but he just might become bereft. TS 18

The man who cannot patiently wait shipwrecks his fate and ends-up imprisoned in self-hate. TS 18

The self-haters are usually the chronic masturbators. TS 18

And who has the ability to ordain the insane so they experience no more psychological and social pain? TS 18

Some people walk a continual contemptuous line that makes it very difficult for them ever to apprehend an opportunity to shine. TS 18

Some people don't want to be part of a team because it would undermine their egocentric schemes. TS 18

You may have met quite the cutie who is a real beauty, however, you'll never be getting some because she'll never get lewdie. TS

Genius is saying much with little; knowing how to widdle; knowing how to fiddle; making killer cakes on the griddle or composing uncrackable riddles. TS 18

Some hateful and useless people are not keen but rather very mean and that's because they need to be weaned from their useless routines that have eroded their self-esteems. TS 17

Don't have a short fuse because you still need to pay your life dues; instead, go have a few killer brews and get renewed rather than live with this internal feud. TS 18

The man who's always deeply sighing is probably internally dying but how many people in reference to his condition are crying for him? TS 18

Having a willful lust might temporarily increase your trust, but soon enough you'll find it's a spiritual bust hence you better get rid of it before you turn to dust. TS 18

A bad loan might turn your heart to stone but maybe you can be shown another way to procure some viable meat-off the bone of your labor by your loving neighbor? TS 18

The wealthy pay a hefty price upon death. TS 18

The masses of people living collective daily lies is a driving force behind understanding why so much good to be realized always dies before it has a chance to fly. TS 18

Only time will tell who in life was truly not well and will be going to an eternal hell; moreover, that *Day of Judgment* will not be swell at the time of the tolling exit bell. TS 18

Those not properly psychologically wired most likely will never get hired but they most certainly will likely get fired. TS 18

Make sure that everything requisite that needs to be said is said before you keel-over dead. TS 18

The world's fart is degrading art. TS 18

The smile of Trini has the magic of Houdini. TS 18

You won't apprehend any life-giving insight when you don't want to take any instruction from those anointed in the light and such a willful ignorant move ain't too bright. TS 18

And what's a greater waste of time than playing church? TS 18

With no fight, insight, and no light, you cannot overcome the blight whose stranglehold is extraordinarily tight. TS 18

The man out of spiritual gas needs a beautiful lass who gives him no sass and has a gorgeous ass! TS 18

The son that has become undone might be perceived as a bum, total scum or mighty dumb; moreover, such scathing criticism might motivate him to get drunkenly numb. TS 18

Not knowing what to do is nothing new and is seldom relegated to only the few. TS 18

The man who's always lying or crying has not the courage of a lion and he surely ain't heading for Zion. TS 18

In this world, there are far more people behaving as Martha rather than Mary, and Jesus's heart breaks because of it. TS 18

Those who are old are cast-out of the accepting fold and into the social cold but those responsible for such unwise actions should be boldly told their lives will never equate to a need for breaking their birth mold. TS 18

I prayed and prayed for the Lord to send someone to minister to me but nobody ever came and how lame that such non-action has forever remained the same? TS 18

At this point, the only motivating energy behind my excellent work is the dignity of my heart. TS 18

The man that has been productive in the worst of situations warrants a dignified and honest worthy responsorial opportunity. TS 18

The person tossed and lost might assume a great cost. TS 18

Identify the incompetent employee to toss lest you suffer a great loss. TS 18

Eventually, frequenting stores and prostitute whores becomes a bore that you just don't want to apprehend anymore. TS 18

The man unwilling to understand is living in social quicksand. TS 18

The United States: A place replete with egocentric people who chronically masturbate because they cannot get any dates. TS 18

Guys: Repent of your sins and maybe you can become like Clark Kent or become a President. TS 18

There's only so much lustful pleasure you can apprehend until you're perceptually convinced it's just another life dead-end. TS 18

Embrace a new way to live and maybe all your wealth flies away. TS 18

And what's more of a fine in life than a killer dine and totally accounted for productive time that doesn't need a bullshit line? TS 18

A pretty sexy wife might just guarantee a life rife with marital strife. TS 18

And what is more of a sight but the man living with all of his might to remain financial tight so he doesn't have to experience an insolvent future fight in old age that puts him in a debilitating scurrying flight as a result of realizing a homeless plight? TS 18

And how many men are in quite the rush to get some tush that really don't know much, and likewise, will ultimately get crushed because of their hell-bent lust? TS 18

You might know much about the Dow but that doesn't guarantee that your prosperously living right now if you're filthy heart motivates you to live like a sow that's always cutting farts while living just on Pop-Tarts. TS 18

The baptism of loneliness is an emptiness that seems bottomless, yet it truly really is the foundation for greatness. TS 18

And how many ignorant selfish people really need a wake-up call or a kick in the shins or getting punched in the chin or some boils on their skin in order to overcome their greedy sins? TS 18

The person who cannot embrace and climb-up the status pegs ends-up in the social dregs. TS 18

There once was a man named Harrell who was married to a gal named Carol but he took a bad fall chasing after a football and now their once beautiful life is in the bottom of the barrel. TS 18

There once was a man named Richard Hyer who crashed his car because of a blown front tire causing it to become on fire and now his life is in the mire. TS 18

The bankruptcy of pleasure knows no measure but being the lost treasure. TS 18

Some people's daily lives are like sitting in a jail with no access to email or being pummeled by hail or eating daily bread that's stale simply because their life went off the rails as a result of having no confidante pals. TS 18

No rough play and never getting laid might explain why some men become gay. TS 18

Fame and wealth are stealthy liars and that's why some God-fearing men have become friars. TS 18

The man that wears a self-protective fraudulent mask can never truly ask for what he needs and is fearful of being seen completing good deeds, yet what is his life truly but a sad tragedy? TS 18

Some people have quit trying because they know they're surrounded by a bunch of people who are lying that ultimately is related to a lot of people perennially sighing and dying and I ain't lying. TS 18

The girl deft with twerking her natal cleft will never be experiencing some serious debt. TS 18

If you suck the meaning out of life as a result of your prolific hell-bent achievements, then you will still know internal strife because something is still not right. TS 18

Sometimes, our hell-bent idolatrous sins make it difficult to perceive where to newly begin in our quest to win and realize a life without chronic-binding sin. TS 18

Be aware of pursuing the woman who will not be taken leaving your soul forsaken simply because she is the one who solely wants to bring home the bacon rather than be home with you baking. TS 18

For some, their life upon earth has been such a forlorn run with little sun or zero fun leaving their souls completely undone. TS 18

If no one is searching you out in order to minister to you, then it's safe to say the church is dead because they haven't made certain that you have been spiritually fed. TS 18

There's nothing worse than looking upon your son who has resolutely concluded he's done because he has never won or had his own son. TS 18

The man that has never had a true love has a proclivity to be mum. TS 18

The man that has nothing in the bank has the greater propensity to wank. TS 18

For many, sexual fantasy is their preferred reality. TS 18

Redundancy: The intellect killer. TS 18

Enough is enough of these college students not having the right stuff because they're sitting on their duff just wanting fluff that's not even intellectually tough. TS 18

Repent of your sins and realize a life-changing win. TS 18

Be inwardly clean and raise your self-esteem. TS 18

Lord, show me the requisite door that I can open to have spiritually more and transcend this epitomized life bore. TS 18

Eating your Wheaties probably will not prevent you from getting diabetes, but it might just make you courageous enough to ask out that beautiful sweetie and that sure would be a treatie! TS 18

There's only so much smoking and toking you can do until your physical body becomes unglued and a choking, yet that news ain't anything new. TS 18

The curse of old age is that society places those folks in a useless status cage and that's because they're not perceived as the latest rage. TS 18

The sheeples will fall. TS 18

Alone with your fantasy dreams will tear-you-up psychologically and spiritually at the seams. TS 18

If that sweet thing has caught your eye, then you better get motivated to set a fire under your ass to go say "Hi" before she ups and goes by by! TS 18

It's the surviving that's actually killing you. TS 18

Wired and totally uninspired is a bad combination like water and fire. TS 18

Drinking tea will make you pee, but hearing constructive criticism and accepting it with glee will help you see and set you free. TS 18

The girl that's spying and lying will keep your relationship with her dying and you crying. TS 18

Take away a person's faithful friends and he's on his way to a serious dead-end. TS 18

And what's worse than the love of your life getting there too late now because you're too old for her to become your mate? TS 18

The only people that can handle and administer power effectively and judiciously are those who have experienced a career of having their ass handed to them over and over again. TS 18

The fleeting moments of pleasure are the snake's bite. TS 18

With mastery derives inevitable boredom. TS 18

When all pleasure is gone, then you're officially gone. TS 18

The conquistador and marriage is not the sky being blue or ham and Swiss or corned beef on toasted rye with melted mozzarella and kraut. TS 18

"Excellence be damned" they said, and then everyone soon thereafter was found dead. TS 18

I once knew a guy who married another guy named Ken and I guess it was probably because he thought Ken was a 10. TS 18

The sacrifice of your excellent labor should find you some favor. TS 18

Some people can only bunt or punt and that's why they're considered social runts or end-up getting a cardio shunt. TS 18

Some people cannot ask for what they need and that's why they're simply unfit to lead. TS 18

As we go about our life business and journey, our physical bodies are dying but that doesn't mean we shouldn't be trying to find a better way to end all our sighing and crying. TS 18

A passionate kiss serves as pure love's conduit for trust/worthiness. TS 18

Some folk's lives are a hoax. TS 18

The grace of Almighty Father God is inexhaustible and we have to pre-empt our need to receive it from him as we need it. TS 18

The individual with the propensity to sue more than likely nobody has ministered to or asked them out for a soothing brew or two. TS 18

Too much wealth undermines one's spiritual health and destroys one's humble self with stealthy deception and Godly rejection without any exception. TS 18

Today's young generation has gone astray thinking its ok to be gay when in the final analysis of it all, they will have to pay for denying the pleasure of a heterosexual lay. TS 18

Some people have a proclivity for mendacity when they really need a date with electricity. TS 18

It's the greedy insane, the ignorant vain or the completely lame who are usually riding the gravy train. TS 18

I once knew a man named Dave who was very brave but unfortunately, he was somebody's slave and he couldn't be saved from an evil trade for a gorgeous maid. TS 18

Masses of people living their lies need to open their eyes lest they will eternally die. TS 18

The face of the lost man is his living embarrassment and he needs to see it for himself for the compelling disgrace that it truly is. TS 18

The coward perpetually clings to someone but lives no life. TS 18

The unworthy and unqualified appointment is an utter embarrassment for the said appointee candidate. TS 18

For some, running-out of things to do is their Kryptonite. TS 18

In most cases, the genius suffers alone and may not even have a loving home that he can call his own because nobody is gracious enough to throw him a social or economic bone. TS 18

The man that cannot adequately fulfill his assigned task is a strong candidate to reach for his flask. TS 18

Holiness leads to aloneness and who can courageously bear it? TS 18

The hot tempered man is usually the coward who in actuality, is screaming at himself. TS 18

The denial of love is the most heinous act of all. TS 18

Fear and unbelief have captivated my heart. TS 18

Many deceivers are responsible for the large group of unbelievers. TS 18

Many a poor have nothing but their Facebook fantasies. TS 18

Your solutions stand all around you, yet you choose otherwise. TS 18

Old age sets-in when a person no longer perceives him/herself as a sexual being. TS 18

Flirting holds more pleasure than sexual conquest any day. TS 18

The hypocrisy of Chamorro culture knows no bounds. TS 18

It's mathematically true that darkness cannot stand in the light every time into eternity. TS 18

And actually, how many snake oil salesmen physicians fallaciously wearing the white-coat are there? TS 18

Every person should experience what's it's like to create some catastrophic art. TS 18

When you're in the middle of reorganizing yourself from a natural disaster and your friends don't call on you to help, then now you know what love isn't. TS 18

Three flights of concrete stairs of non-lubricant sledding (other than typhoon water) and 40 yards of crawling on tile floor in order to survive, will not be classified by you as an adventure. TS 18

The effectiveness of a natural disaster's clean-up and revitalization effort is related to its geo-physical location and size. TS 18

A little break that's not expected might go a long way toward giving a person a chance to see his life opportunities in a different way than he would never have had the opportunity to embrace. TS 18

And Kaz said to me: "You're no pussy." TS 18

Ass was handed to me and ass was kicked by me so some progress ostensibly was made by me and that's a good thing. TS 18

Making the wrong decisions with the willfully wrong mentality inevitably brings the wrath. TS 18

No one bats 1.000 percent in life. Some things are going to get lost. TS 18

Now that you have no high speed Internet access what are you thinking about now that you either: never thought about or were never going think about? TS 18

Time for smelling the Joe bro because God doesn't want you to be a homo or to utterly blow, he wants you to be in the total know. TS 18

The *off-the-beaten path life* is the life that can really become artistically productive for prolific sakes. TS 18

The crown of the perennially suffering man is honored courage that has been purely earned. TS 18

Italian sausage is one of the best things to happen in life. TS 18

When Almighty God is saying "Be still and know that I am God" that doesn't necessarily mean whatever he is planning is going to turn-out the way you want it to turn-out. TS 18

If after a complete destruction of your community by a cataclysmic super typhoon all your friend can say to you is: I want to go work-out at Gold's Gym and I wonder if its open, then you now know the essence of egocentric idiocy. TS 18

If someone is half-listening to you all of the time when you talk to him, then he isn't your friend; however, he just might be someone that would lead you to a dead-end. TS 18

Until you have watched the front door of your home consumed by 200 mile hour winds what is that you think you know? TS 18

The natural world has primacy over humankind and will implements its own will accordingly as it sees fit with no regard for people's status, prestige, wealth, race, ethnicity, gender, education, etc. TS 18

We walk a fine line between stability versus calamity 24/7 and we are not even cognizant of this fact as we bitch over petty life matters. TS 18

Calamities are a great social leveler too. TS 18

For some people, the highlight of their day is having access to some soap and a shower. TS 18

Create some typhoon art from your destroyed life that's been thrown apart and now know more than in part. TS 18

It is true that the karma of the earth's natural powerful forces are ready to punish humanity for its willful sins of injustice, apathy and unrighteous at Almighty God's behest at any time. TS 18

Seeking clarity of purpose is a good thing, but truthfully know if you're on that quest, that will be taking a few dings from the evil spirit world for attempting to become more helpful and powerful as a result of increased understanding of purpose. TS 18

It is true that Almighty God can throw humankind back into the stone-age at any time so don't become too arrogant in reference to what you have regarding wealth or what you have so-called achieved. TS 18

The sedentary life of routine is the slow death that emanates without cognitive awareness; and in many cases, the cumulative losses that are piling-up in the meanwhile of such an existence will suddenly explode like a sleeping volcano and wreak havoc upon such a person. TS 18

Maybe life's greatest tragedies regarding humanity's story is a lack of perceptual awareness of the present and future and an inability to remember the past. TS 18

If you're exhausted and you're still doing viable work, then you're a worthy first round pick. TS 18

How can anyone say love is lust? TS 18

Most of us die in our habits and never change even though we know we should change. TS 18

If you know its idiocy and a waste of time, then the Lord has to know it also. TS 18

When we make reference to the *power of a statement*, then we are identifying its impact and pervasiveness. TS 18

As long as you have a place to take a shit, you're doing alright. TS 18

All this time you have lived, you have lost track of a plethora of minutes, hours and days that you have experienced both good and bad; and the tragedy is that you cannot have all of them in front of you when you're living in the present-tense in order to either help you make more effective decisions or to keep you from contemplating self-destruction. TS 18

When Almighty God is saying "Be Still and Know that I am God" is he saying that because he has hope for your future or he knows that you have no future? TS 18

Dealing with any point of crisis or destruction requires the ability to be a methodical builder who invests the necessary energy to lay one brick at a time. TS 18

Praise Almighty Lord God for contemplation time in order to comprehend how vain and ignorant humankind really is along with the fact that you are a part of that vanity and ignorance as well. TS 18

If you are great, it's only because the Holy Spirit of grace and power is the author of your greatness, and if there is any credit due to you, it's the fact that you have allowed the Holy Spirit to do his work in you. TS 18

The possibilities that exist for the creation of your life journey are the miracle itself and here you are bitching about the view. TS 18

Nobody is pure and don't deceive yourself otherwise. TS 18

Humanity's train wreck is that nobody is pure in thought and action 100% of the time and that is why the human race advances at a snail's pace from generation to generation. TS 18

Geophysical time and space separation is the enemy of human empathy. TS 18

The individual that can endure aloneness now has some real productive possibilities for his/her life. TS 18

The babies are the light of the world so don't be a fool and ignore that reality thereby blinding yourself from seeing what truly matters in this life. TS 18

If you have not had an opportunity to hug and kiss your own baby deriving from your flesh and blood, then unfortunately, you have missed-out on a great blessing. TS 18

Life is a very short ride so make sure by the time you reach mid-life that you have achieved something noteworthy enough to underscore that you didn't waste your time because when old age arrives, you will be focusing on staying alive not on being productive. TS 18

Before you get pissed-off toward someone for his/her betrayal or abandonment against you, consider the fact that their behavior is motivated more by weakness than hatred or apathy toward you. TS 18

If you know how to spend money when you need to spend money, then you're on the way to setting the foundation of your success regardless of how much you have available to spend. TS 18

The blowhard is the vain and ignorant person whose presence reeks with foolishness and he's an embarrassment to himself and he doesn't even know it. TS 18

The man without tenderness and mercy loses big time and maybe if he had some tenderness and mercy shown to him, he could do likewise? TS 18

Some men are thinking they need another bottle in order to motivate their throttle, but maybe they really need to be coddled? TS 18

Access to the inexhaustible supply of Almighty God's strength is available to us, however, we have to willfully ask for it. TS 18

Life on the run certainly is no fun and the chance to be productive loses by the ton henceforth circumventing opportunities for many life victories and souls to be won. TS 18

The person who is sorely sick might be at the end of his/her wick so he/she doesn't need a hateful kick, but for you to be his/her encouraging brick in order to build healing hope and help him/her tick. TS 18

Every day on earth is another miracle for you to apprehend. TS 18

The dead-end of the carnal mind knows no limits. TS 18

Planning is requisite but planning defers to nature. TS 18

The vicissitudes of life and their energy are surely hell-bent and will certainly make a dent to make one spent, but as long as he can still pay the rent, he won't have to live in a tent wondering where all of his money went? TS 18

Nature will make sure there is no human plan that will permanently take hold to alter its course. TS 18

Nature has her own will and she will take back from humankind all that we have taken from her. TS 18

Smoking meth is the slow death. TS 18

I remember this dude who was talking shit about me buying cheap trinkets in reference to the places that I had visited. Now he's dead and I still have my cheap trinkets that outlasted him. TS 18

Don't mock cheap trinkets, they may outlast you. TS 18

Any vestiges that uphold atheism will be laid waste by Almighty Lord God in his time as he see fit. Tis a certainty. TS 18

Nature periodically provides the douching humankind needs in reference to its behavioral ways that lead to nothing worthy. TS 18

And how many truly holy people exist in this world that actually have power to heal other people and help them become holy and of exceptional vocational utility? TS 18

Having some gold is a big help when you need to fight back and do well, and if you truthfully and justifiably earned it through your natural abilities and hard work, then people bitching about you and your welfare can go to hell. TS 18

Leave the man in peace who has earned his keep and then you'll make certain you will not pay a price too steep for persecuting him with your cheap and useless intellect. TS 18

The rife poverty of Manila Metro is the earth's anus. TS 18

Those people living life everyday to secure their ability to remain the same are surely pretty lame and quite the mighty shame because in actuality, their lives are in chains. TS 18

Being 56 years-old living in poverty is quite lame and it will not be placing you in life's hall of fame but maybe rather the hall of shame. TS 18

And how do you operationally define what it means to be psychotic? It is the homeless man who walks down the street with the same clueless expression on his face that he always wore prior to a mass typhoon that ran through his community and that same face he is still wearing now after that mass typhoon just tore his community a new asshole. TS 18

One aspect of social change is suffering and if you have a long-life journey, you will certainly be knowing that reality; moreover in many cases, there will be no dress rehearsal for what you will be suffering in those unrehearsed social change experiences. TS 18

Acrimony in your heart won't open doors to Almighty God's heart on your behalf. TS 18

Limited empathy in humankind's collective heart is why this race of a creation is still in the stone-age. TS 18

Only vanity projects into the future believing everything will assuredly turn-out as expected. TS 18

The aimless man with no purpose has too much time to think about all of the bad that he can do. TS 18

What has primarily set this globe back in the last hundred years is too many people having limited opportunities for self-actualization due to horrible living conditions, limited infrastructure development, limited higher education and skill development and diverse languages. TS 18

The slow death is having nothing meaningful to do. TS 18

Catastrophic natural disasters suffered multiple times by a respective community is the Sisyphus Syndrome. TS 18

Don't berate the person weary of his/her life ass-beating when you have never taken one yourself. TS 18

Vain imaginations keep people running toward a direction that leads to the bottomless pit. TS 18

Bitching only matters if all things are to remain socially constant in order for desired change to occur somewhere down the line. TS 18

Social upheaval will maybe make a vain man become an insane man as a result of losing his wealth, his status and consistent lifestyle that props-up his vain and insane ways. TS 18

Like coal and what intense pressure creates it to be, is how we must learn how to be so we can permanently do good deeds. TS 18

Man's strength doesn't last and nature or Almighty God can break-it quickly. TS 18

The inevitable will of social change to be wrought has its own will like typhoon force winds and it will take over as it sees fit. TS 18

Maybe much of your suffering has its origins in your lack of self-confidence or your unwillingness to be vain or both? TS 18

A strike is the withholding of energy to complete a goal. Many people go on a strike such as: mothers; fathers; agricultural laborers; unionized laborers; husbands; wives; sons; daughter; students; teachers; garbage workers; pastors; lovers; friends, etc. TS 18

Almighty God can lay waste to anything, but if he does so, then what is it that he wants in return from the people that had what surrounds them laid waste to? TS 18

Most people live their lives upon this earth never knowing pure love as a giver and/or receiver and that underscore the tragedy of their lives. TS 18

I said it before, nature is no respecter of persons; your status cannot save you from a deadly hailstorm or typhoon. TS 18

What's worse than being physically injured and having no vocational direction in addition to that? TS 18

The tragedy and fallibility of the human individual is he cannot completely remember where he has been and what he has experienced. TS 18

Anyone can manage when he is at his best, but what about after he has had his legs cut-off or had a block fall upon his head? How effectively will he manage now? TS 18

The sexually perverted mind is extraordinarily difficult to eradicate because its selling point is based upon: What will purity do for me but leave me socially alone? TS 18

The missionary slave is like the neglected household pet that everyone forgets. TS 18

The good man watches everyone flee from his presence and his life is cursed with zero intimacy and zero understanding. TS 18

If you watch Almighty God destroy a church, then you certainly have every right to be completely flummoxed about what his true intentions are regarding anything that supposedly sustains life. TS 18

Be of good cheer and be aware; not even the world's greatest sage who is the rage that's taking center stage can stop a cataclysmic happening from moving this generation of people back into the Stone Age. TS 18

"Excellence be damned!" the local community college hiring committee exclaimed! TS 18

Vain pretension rules the land and that's why the nation is actually sinking in quicksand. TS 18

Freedom day is not July 4th 1776, it's the day that you physically die and leave this oppressive earth. TS 18

No respect yields no tenderness. TS 18

Egocentrism has a tendency to increase with old age simply because the needs for caring for your physical and psychological health become greater as part of the aging process along with striving to stay vocationally relevant. TS 18

It is true that some people's lives will have a horrible ending. Likewise, pray that you're not part of that litany list. TS 18

For some souls when their life race has been run, it will not have been a lot of fun, but hopefully, Almighty Father God will reward them a hefty ton as a result of so much in their earthly life not being won. TS 18

And who was that beautiful young girl in my dream that said to me so boldly – "just kiss me because I know you want to kiss me." Boy, I wish I knew who she was. TS 18

So much in life fights against our dignity as we proceed through the life cycle stages and we never completely know whether those experiences and factors are from an evil source or a good source. Nevertheless, our lack of clarity in reference to the source that drives such powerful energy doesn't make us feel any better about ourselves, and in some instances, might even push us over the edge. TS 18

So many educated persons in today's world rue having nothing meaningful to do because those who are in power with less education are afraid of anyone who can say "boo!" and unfortunately, that's nothing new - just ask the Jews. TS 18

Love may cover a multitude of sins, but it doesn't prevent those who are in the world with no love in their hearts from their sinning. TS 18

Only a jackass who lives through a super typhoon says afterward, "It was an adventure." TS 18

Some of the people in life that need your help will never be getting your help and that's the unfortunate truth for them. TS 18

So I had a dream about a famous black crooner who everyone was saying had the greatest voice you ever had to hear. When I and the beautiful girl I was with found him, he was laying on his back with his ass in the air. So what is that supposed to mean? TS 18

Without utilities, the detailed plans can never be realized. TS 18

If you're having a dream about your false teeth falling out, what does that mean? TS 18

What good is it to evolve into a higher level of understanding if nobody can understand what you now understand? TS 18

If you're in crisis after a natural disaster has wiped-out your home, and you ask you brother to call you and he doesn't, then what does that mean? TS 18

The excellence of teaching is not related to the eloquent sound of your articulated voice but how *relevant and accurate it is in reference to* what you're attempting to teach. TS 18

What do we call a place where we receive no love and encouragement ever? It is called *hell* my friends. TS 18

Fearing the person that knows more than you is an unwise move and you lose out as you move away from such an individual because now, there is so much that you're never going to learn that you could have learned. TS 18

Inspiring art should be teaching current and future generations of people about belief systems that maintain and evolve lives of success and achievement that relate to sustaining life and regarding it as sacred. TS 18

And how many people have you known over the years that fell off the face of the earth because apparently, they didn't see enough value in your personhood to continue on in a path of knowing you? TS 18

And how many people will be dying today and you will not be there to lay eyes upon that experience; however, you not being there isn't going to prevent them from not checking-out. TS 18

Your inability to remember how relevant all of what you have learned currently influences the proficiency of what you behave today in reference to your vocation, and actually assails your dignity to be all of what you should be in reference to knowing factual truth about yourself, and that's certainly not helpful. TS 18

What do you think you know or can endure until you have tried to sleep at night in Saipan without any AC in 100% relative humidity? TS 18

Bottom-line is most people who are in charge of things are weak cowards who will do everything in their power to keep their status of being in so-called charge; yet in reality, they're useless cowards. A sad fact indeed and yet this phenomena is happening all-across the world and has been for centuries. TS 18

When nobody wants your help anymore, then I guess it's time to die. TS 18

It's been 3 years and 3 months since Hurley mumbled underneath his breath as he passed me by that "Nobody Cares," and truly, the evidence of what the man stated is abundantly clear in factual support of his utterance. Sad indeed! TS 18

Every day is an opportunity for doing good or showering someone with love, yet how many people are missing that boat every day as well? TS 18

What's behind the asshole's ignorant way of life is his vanity. TS 18

Until you have had your home destroyed by a natural disaster, what the hell is it that you said you think you know? TS 18

Hilarious that Americans are beating their chests claiming America is the greatest country upon earth while all they can muster for their National Presidency are frauds like Mr. Oblama and Mr. Trump. Sad indeed. TS 18

Those with no hope usually have an impending date with the soap. TS 18

Jesus warned against the uselessness of chasing after and collecting mammon, yet what are we doing but worshiping people like Warren Buffett and the New York Stock Exchange. TS 18

The man with a long scar from a super typhoon deserves to hear a happy tune and see the best of days in his life coming real soon! TS 18

Be of good cheer; you could have a brother and mother that don't give druthers about your comfort and are unwilling to share or express any care in order to secure your welfare. TS 18

Every day there are a lot of people not even trying, sighing and dying, and I ain't lying. TS 18

For some people, their dual legacy will be they were not lazy and they were not crazy. TS 18

If you're not known and all alone, it's more than likely nobody is going to be throwing you a bone or buying you an ice cream cone, yet that just might motivate you to go and get stoned. TS 18

This earth offers very little mirth but it does indeed offer much dearth in reference to anything of lasting worth. TS 18

The man that's totally bored shouldn't fall upon his sword, he should buy an F-150 Pickup Ford and find the Lord in order to have something to look forward toward. TS 18

The man that shows mercy is the greatest man. TS 18

No empathy = no mercy. TS 18

The idolatry of the life of ease that's a breeze experienced by the selfish is what ultimately brings the suffering poor to their knees. TS 18

If you cannot see the good that you are in reference to what you're potentially capable of achieving with what you have been endowed, then you will spend your life getting psychologically plowed by the mass crowd who doesn't give damn whether you're well-endowed. TS 18

The teacher that doesn't take on mentees to build the *learned tree* so others can eventually see is not functioning as a portal of entry key. TS 18

The foremost fact that must be recalled first in reference to the character and behavior of Almighty God is he is sovereign and therefore, that is why he is Almighty God and you are not and never will be. Forget this fact as a foundation for your supposed rational thinking, and you're on the wrong road in reference to many of the conclusions you derive. TS 18

The tragedy of time that moves forward is all that you have forgotten that you probably really need in your present-tense to remember for the betterment of your welfare. TS 18

And so much of what the wise man knows never finds its way to those who need that information the most and that is a twofold problem related to: 1) too few wise men, and 2) too many people that don't care to know. TS 18

The man who is chickless that goes stickless is by no means feckless. TS 18

No one really can imagine that they truly are going to die and realize an eternal by by - so before you do - make sure you eat some of Grandma's killer apple pie. TS 18

The cruel and unusual punishment associated with capital punishment is a last meal cheeseburger without pickle. TS 18

Too much time on a person's hands make him/her use those hands in other ways to pass the time in a pleasurable manner. TS 18

For some unfortunate souls, it's time for a nifty cleft-liftee. TS 18

Insanity has a great chance to take hold in one's life after he has done all that is required and beyond that, yet all of the wrong results follow suit 100% of the time! TS 18

For the chicks that don't want to have sex anymore or no one wants to have sex with them anymore, their next choice for pleasure is usually food. TS 18

The life of purity is a complete bore as long as you still have a physical body that has its origins in so-called original sin. TS 18

When the norm of your life has become coping and that is the norm that you now prefer, then it's now time for Almighty God to perform the miracle upon your lost self. TS 18

Some people are not worth talking to because they truly will never change their ways in reference to using you to fulfill their personal goals with no thanks ever forwarded toward you regardless. TS 18

The achiever has the most difficult time understanding the relevance of submitting and resting in the belief that Almighty God will see goodwill to fruition. TS 18

The life of zero meaningful consistent intimacy does indeed suck and no big bucks or fast-fuck will make it not ever suck. TS18

You should have some life-long artifacts to surround you that document the meaning of your life while you're living as well as when you're dying. TS 18

Lord, have mercy upon us and inspire us to be thankful for life itself and find the examples of what we need to be grateful for on a daily basis – minute by minute, hour by hour, day by day and year to year. TS 18

The thankful heart is revived. TS 18

The boss should be the one that knows what to do every day. TS 18

So many souls trying to find a way out of the daily grind that's so unkind and leaves many lives in a daily bind and is fostered along by selfish and greedy people in power who are completely spiritually blind. TS 18

And what person can stay completely pure and utterly see clearly with no blur thereby having the power to live life fully cured? TS18

Pray that the tsunami of chaos that unknowingly is ultimately pending doesn't find you in order to either debilitate you or ruin you. TS 18

And where is the love of God to be found in social and economic life destruction? TS 18

And who are those people running the governments of the nations in this world but the untrustworthy, the vain and the ignorant while you have stupid people believing that voting is going to make it better when the same types of former people mentioned are the candidates on the ballot. TS 18

The curse of achievement is never being satisfied with the achievements. See Solomon. TS 18

The life prepared for hell as his home resides in hot as hell Saipan. TS 18

And how many people are faithfully waiting for the miracle that will never come? TS 18

We endure to cope but also to inevitably overcome the coping so we can stop moping and doping. TS 18

Some people need to be boldly told in order to break their dysfunctional mold of being deceptively sold lest they spend their lives out in the abandoned cold. TS 18

Building steeples doesn't keep unqualified people from defrauding the mass sheeples. TS18

A pristine living routine cannot ultimately guarantee a life of continual esteem or ending-up on the best team, but it just might lead to someone getting reamed and creamed. TS 18

Weary and angry is a killer combination. TS 18

When they're calling you a doctor and you don't even have your PhD, then why do you need a PhD? TS 18

Many marriages burn-out on love, and unfortunately in many cases, it's like a spent candle. TS 18

The one talking the most might have a lot to prove; however, too much garrulous behavior is perceived as a sign of stupidity. TS 18

And then she saw me, and there she was again making the effort to stand in front of me. Thank God! TS 18

And how many people get married, and then, the love of their life arrives later on down the line? TS 18

And the guy was talking like he was in charge and he was the man, yet little did he know that the future held for him a super typhoon; and when it struck - he was outta here like a coward! Classic. TS 18

Unbelief kept Jesus in the dregs and is doing so now for many of us. TS 18

Catastrophe wipes-out arrogance and tears it a new asshole. TS 18

A little bit of REM sleep regenerates the degenerate soul toward hope. TS 18

If you cannot remember anything else worth a damn, then remember that gravity reigns. TS 18

The guy that's had 8 jobs in 8 years is probably a snake oil salesman. TS 18

No one can do good 24/7 and that's the Devil's stronghold to undermine the human race. TS 18

If people don't consistently treat you well, then it's more than likely your psychological disposition is heading for hell. TS 18

2018 was a great year: I lost all of my four bottom front teeth; was offered a $80,000 dollar a year job and then had the offer rescinded; I had a staph infection on my back for a month and then was almost killed in a super typhoon three months later six days before my birthday. And now, I have to somehow keep believing that Almighty God epitomizes love, when in fact, my 33-year-old Bible was water-logged destroyed, along with a beautiful picture of my father and me. TS 18

Jesus said that he had no place to lay his head and some good intentioned souls living now will someday find out what it's like to have no bed as they are on their way to being treated like they're dead. TS 18

When your own immediate and extended blood family doesn't offer to help you after suffering through a calamitous event, now you know what love is not. TS 18

Stay well or go to hell. TS 18

Men, don't feel guilty about your sexual needs; these needs are purely physiological responses associated with your maleness and you had nothing to do with deciding to be a male before you were born. TS 18

It's not the great blue whale that's going extinct, rather it's the great white male going extinct. TS 18

Think about how you want to have your life end: suddenly without warning birthing forth a quick exit, or a slow demise that might involve some long-term suffering, yet warrants you the time to get your so-called affairs in order? TS 18

There was life before the Internet and there will be life long after the Internet is gone in Jesus' new kingdom upon earth. Thank Almighty Lord God for that! TS 18

Looking at your smartphone all day long while you ignore the world around you isn't an example of a person lead by the Holy Spirit. See Christ's living behavioral example if you doubt it. TS 18

It's the mercy and grace of Almighty Father God that keeps us all alive whether we believe or know it or not. TS 18

And we certainly do not receive the punishment for our sins as we deserve just as the Holy Scriptures testify; for instance, how many sins are we committing in our hearts that are replete with perversion, idolatry and hate or how many willful sins our we committing in reference to hatred, cowardice, and disobedience in comparison to what we are supposed to be behaviorally doing, etc.? A contemplated time of mediation will reveal how unworthy we truly are to be amongst the living in order to experience the pleasures and blessings of life bestowed upon us from Almighty Father God, and it will do us good to comprehend how much we have willfully taken for granted so we may humbly ask Almighty Father God for his forgiveness and mercy. TS 18

Does a man's parents love him when they ignore his birthday and don't even follow-up with him after he has survived a super typhoon that almost killed him? TS 18

Love expressed through words is extraordinarily impotent. TS 18

Great health motivates egocentric folly, yet debilitated health might produce far more focused utilitarian productive results in one's life. TS 18

The parents that could not show love to their children will be held accountable by Almighty God for their derelict duty and that will be a sad hearing to attend. TS 18

The forlorn soul is the shame of this earthly life. TS 18

There are too many people in the USA running around with their unqualified higher education degrees earned via lame non-rigorous academic institutions thereby devaluing all higher education degrees and obscuring the criteria determining who is truly qualified to hold specific types of employment. TS 18

If you want to destroy a person's will to live, then give him nothing to do worth a damn. TS 18

All this scurrying around and then it's here and gone and nowhere to be found as the earth gets the last laugh as it consumes its inhabitants one by one on a daily basis. TS 18

The soul that remains scantily touched by trouble and suffering learns little and has no worthiness to lead other persons toward any truly profitable end. TS 18

The *living death* is treading water for years in your career dead-end because nobody will rightfully give you the chance you deserve because of either jealousy, fear or hate. TS 18

Why are you apologizing for something you vehemently said (that you care passionately about) in order to appease the minority of people that don't agree with you? TS 18

There is no individual that I have ever met in this life that actually believes there is a plan in the midst of social chaos. TS 18

Whether you want to believe it or not or like it or not, the massive economic inequities of income in the USA aren't something that Almighty God is pleased with; therefore, why are people surprised that he has been bombarding relentless cataclysmic disasters upon that nation over the last generation? TS 18

The problem of the emptiness in one's soul has been going on since the beginning of living creation and will never end until life as we know it ends. TS 18

And where have all of the molecules of collective historical human thought gone-off to? TS 18

If at mid-life, you cannot think of anything else to say, maybe it's because you have led many productive days and don't see the need to embrace any other ways of contemplation and beliefs. TS 18

Don't be deceived, even the holy man needs pleasure. TS 18

The man of light is always in a constant fight to overcome the plight of the masses of souls whose lives are completely uptight as a result of refusing to live right. TS 18

And think of how many people that surround you that you'll truly never know, and yet, even though you will never know them, they believe their lives matter whether you know them or not? TS 18

I don't have a problem believing in the existence of God, I have a problem believing in the love of God. TS 18

If you're living like a consistent louse maybe then you'll end-up with a mouse in your house so don't grouse. TS 18

The people that don't confess usually have more stress and sleep less. TS 18

And how many people's lives resemble the scurrying ant revolving around in peripatetic motion? TS 18

Why is Almighty God chastising you for unbelief in him when he doesn't answer your prayers, help you or intercede on your behalf for your welfare? Bizarre. TS 18

If Almighty God would be a little more kind, empathetic and helpful rather than jealous for people turning to other sources for survival, coping and pleasure, then maybe he would get a little more love. TS 18

The people who are praising Almighty God the loudest are the ones with the easiest ass lives. TS 18

Arrogance loses its pants when denied a second chance. TS 18

Some people love their dope in order to cope, but that's probably the better choice than the rope. TS 18

The grand evolvement of the collective human race is really an impossibility simply because of the multitudinous language barriers. Sorry. TS 18

Take away a man's access to utilities and he's a now going a nowhere fast. TS 18

The earth has its own will and is no respecter of people's homes, wealth, assets or status. TS 18

Not everyone can rebuild from the ashes of their former lives and those who are able are the most courageous and capable of leading. TS 18

Mid-life and old age is primarily about celibacy and it's not because that's what you want. TS 18

Some things have the potential to be very good, yet can have the opposite effect where they can be very bad: See fire, water, wind and marriage if you doubt it. TS 18

The genius is on the precipice of utter clarity versus insanity all of the time. TS 18

When death is upon his hell-bent warpath to take you, he will find you and take you lest Almighty God intercedes on your behalf. TS 18

It's all chemistry. TS 18

For the Godly man, remember that the Son of Man had no place to lay his head so be prepared for the street to possibly become your bed. TS 18

The vicissitudes of life may offer rife experiences of strife that cut like a knife, but try to overcome them by being a person that does not let them make you uptight. TS 18

Chasing after fleeting fame is completely lame so make sure you didn't miss the life-giving bus that has already came. TS 18

The many souls with a limited vocational lot will inevitably sit and rot. TS 18

The only plan that truly matters is the one that makes the world perfect in social/economic harmony, utility and love. Anything less is a true waste of time. TS 18

You're truly less of a person because of your inept ability to remember all that has occurred in your life – for the good and for the bad. TS 18

If you want to be perennially kicked in the can, then reside in Saipan. TS 18

Maybe those people who love to commit sodomy need a lobotomy? TS 18

Vanity always has a huge cost that may not be immediately knowable. TS 18

I know a guy who's always talking about studying his religious books, yet he's the most self-absorbed egocentric person alive. So what is the religion he is studying called? Egocentrism assholism? TS 18

It's amazing how many people upon this earth are wealthy for doing things of little or no value in reference to securing equity and justice. Total joke. TS 18

Unfortunately, as relevant as money is for sustenance, it defiles everything in that process. TS 18

One of my 18-year old students said that her natural talent is sleeping. Now talk about someone that has had little contemplation time or worthy social encouragement. TS 18

The man of truth and clarity as his consistent disposition is the first asset you should recruit and retain in order to build your team. TS 18

Those people who are running from the truth are not your friends. TS 18

Talk is meaningless. So why don't you sit your ass down in the heart of poverty and see what your talk does about eradicating poverty? Total joke. TS 18

What's so *royal* about people who are going to die? Total deception. TS 18

The man that can make consistent accurate decisions while he's physically and psychologically exhausted is your first round pick. TS 18

And what does it really come down to in the final analysis of things but that people desire for all to be secure in their present and future lives, and yet, who can find blame with that? TS 18

And what is power but something fleeting that leaves behind mass destruction. TS 18

The curse of the earth is that thralldom in reference to those physical bodies that inhabit it that are sentenced to suffering in their quest for survival. TS 18

Being good doesn't prevent you from suffering or having injustices imposed upon you; if anything, it probably heightens the distribution of both of those experiences. TS 18

The flawed theology of American Christianity is the belief that Almighty God owes his creation something in reference to their existence. TS 18

In all honesty, I'm the second son in the Prodigal Son story who came in from the field wondering, "What the hell is going on?" TS 18

I don't need a smartphone or a loan or a lawyer; I need a miracle. TS 18

All of this sitting around is going to put me in the ground. TS 18

One primary cost of technological advancement is social irrelevance. TS 18

Remember people, you cannot make love to your smartphone, but you can damn well try! TS 18

It's just like Bob Jaworski said in 1984: "I'm too hip for the straight crowd and too straight for the hip crowd." TS 18

Nevertheless, it's time for a world political enema. TS 18

Build your own nation economical strong and politically just and your people will have no need or desire to go anywhere else. TS 18

Why get a PhD degree if people are already calling you Doctor Whatever? TS 18

Don't begrudge anyone the easy life - especially if he has worked hard and earned it! TS 18

The perfect life doesn't exist because change is the norm of nature, and nature is predominant over humankind. TS 18

The futility with so many religions in their attempt to explain the origins of an Almighty God or a supernatural power or why injustice reigns over good is like a person groping to find the toilet in the pitch dark. TS 18

If you have some clarity toward comprehending the social reality that surrounds you, then you're doing well and probably have better mental health because of it. TS 18

Some people's life sentence is social rejection and they can never get out of it. TS 18

Jesus said the world will readily throw-out the chief capstone so maybe that explains why you have been consistently thrown-out during the course of your life-time. TS 18

I once knew a guy named Sammy who wanted to start a family with a girl named Tammy but he fell on his head getting out of bed and now he's financially in the red thereby suffering from this double-whammy. TS 18

If you're feeling guilty about your extramarital desires that are undermining your current sexual desires for the person that you said you would take care of for all-time, then you need to get yourself together before you start a nasty living fire. TS 18

Experiencing physiological pain and simultaneously having a zero vocational plan is the double-whammy of living insane. TS 18

What else can be said when you're living in a dead-end and nobody around you will lovingly lend or willingly bend to help you get on the mend? TS 18

Don't die in your sins because you couldn't find any faith to believe that Almighty God and love is good or you'll end-up not the way you lovingly should be. TS 18

Only time will tell what despicable souls are going to be sentenced to hell but make sure to leave a legacy of doing good in order to secure that you're eternally well. TS 18

What do you think you know about anything until you have had to try to sleep in 100% relative humidity for days upon end without AC? TS 18

Keep fighting your fight to be the light but soberly realize few people will regard you as a *White Knight,* yet that's because their life plight is not being able to recognize the light and that's why they continue to live amidst the blight. TS 18

Somewhere down the line, mercy will relent and you will finally be sent to make the ultimate dent against evil for goodness's sake. TS 18

Don't lust to become a leader because in your vain ignorance, you truly don't know the steep price that must personally be paid in order to procure that status title. TS 18

Bankruptcy of the heart is like a ranking fart, yet it can be overcome with a kick in the bum or a shot of rum so don't remain living as scum. TS 18

Living blind as a bat will make you live like a rat that's always taking a crap. TS 18

Your creative potential lies within you like magma waiting to come to the surface and become lava. TS 18

Some people are like clueless shrews that don't know how to live anything new and all they want to do is chew and go to the loo. TS 18

The question is: when we die, do we remember who we were in this earthly life or is that memory obliterated? TS 18

If you're habitually cursing the hellish circumstances that you've had unwittingly cast upon your life, then remember that lesser people would have already blown their brains-out! TS 18

The *out-of-sight* mentality rules and who can contend with it? TS 18

If you have been assailed, nailed and impaled and in the meanwhile your friends have bailed, then now you know the abandonment and crucifixion of Christ. TS 18

Photos capture the moment but never the complete story behind the image. TS 18

There actually maybe victory in misery, yet who can really see it? TS 18

Yesterday's gone and it cannot be altered; and for some, that is the best news possible, and for others, it's the worst news possible. TS 18

Change in the geophysical world is the norm and yet we seldom learn any lessons from this fact; instead, much of our planning and logic is based upon creating personal security and stable social, economic and technological systems, when in reality, change is the norm and will ultimately undermine all of the plans we have made to achieve any form of security and stability. TS 18

Self-control is motivated by the pure heart and mind and that is not something truly and consistently achievable by the aggregate human race. TS 18

The surest way to irrelevance is to die in a sudden natural disaster. TS 18

The good thing about the fact that you have evolved into a place of being non-materialistic and adaptable to change is now you can endure the powerful and hateful vicissitudes of surviving a natural disaster and not be suicidal. TS 18

Positions of strength are fleeting, so likewise, be prepared for the greeting of a serious future ass-beating. TS 18

You may be out of physical or psychological gas but that may not indicate that's because you're an ass, so instead, make an effort to fast and maybe you can receive a pass that will help you last. TS 18

The strength of Almighty Lord God sustains you, yet many have no clue of what to do in order to gain access to that power in their most difficult hours. TS 18

You may not be a tower of power, but you might certainly be in need of a shower. TS 18

I once knew a young man named Michael who loved to recycle but he was so ignorant he didn't even know how to ride a bicycle. TS 18

Don't forsake the artist because he may offer you counsel and instruction in a manner that would have never reached you with what you absolutely need to know. TS 18

And how many adult people on earth are functioning as non-sexual beings and that's not by their choice? TS 18

And how many people need just anyone to preempt a "Hi" so they don't collapse and die? TS 18

Some people will end-up dead before they're ever wed or spiritually fed and led. TS 18

And what a tragedy for the old lady that never learned to love another human being in an intimate way, yet her dog is her only willful loving option for realizing a blessed day. TS 18

The person who cannot accept or give a loving hug, might actually need a punch in the mug. TS 18

Be aware: The person who was consistently picked last for Dodge Ball when you were a kid, might end-up leading you all. TS 18

Pray to Almighty God that you don't have a kid who thinks it's all a crock of shid. TS 18

Don't be surprised that the genius has no real friends; if that's so, it's because he knows most people and their stupid ways are just dead-end yoyos. TS 18

The man that longs and wishes for a passionate kiss, yet gets constantly dissed, understandably gets pissed! TS 18

Fantasies in the heart are all some people have to keep them from falling apart so don't be so quick to call them retarts. TS 18

And who has the temerity to confront unjust austerity and communicate about its debilitating forces with complete clarity? TS 18

We delude ourselves to believe that everything is in order, yet utterly forgetting that nature is primary over man and may completely flip us and our pretty homes right on our can! TS 18

If you have anything worthy to leave behind, then let it be known that you were mighty kind. TS 18

If you're too tired to get inspired, then maybe you'll end-up getting fired and that will actually help you become unwired so you won't be so damn tired. TS 18

After Almighty God destroys your home, tell me what it is you're supposed to believe in? TS 18

Why would an omniscient God see fit to sacrifice a person's debilitated present life in association with building his soul toward holiness along with the social and psychological mess it creates for himself and others when this is less than a perfect solution? TS 18

Maybe our notion of a perfect omniscient God is not correct although he may be very close to perfect. TS 18

A dearth of love causes many social and psychological ills that cannot be eradicated by pharmacological pills or alcohol producing stills. TS 18

The fleshly life upon earth is a NY Minute yet because people are utterly clueless of what exists beyond death this fact alone primarily explains why most people's time and energy is completely invested in this temporary earthly life. TS 18

As ignorant and vain as I am, that does not preclude me from taking note of what to be thankful for as a part of my daily meditative exercise. TS 18

We spend all of this time, energy and money on pampering ourselves in order to realize temporary health and comfort, and then, it all comes crashing down regardless of our so-called justified, intelligent or loving efforts. TS 18

Some people will spend their entire lives never going without access to electricity and water and thereby will never comprehend the fortitude of billions of courageous and powerful souls that preceded them who endured a life of constant and complete hardship; and likewise, they will be truly inferior and weak as a result of their life of ignorant ease. TS 18

If Almighty God has a plan for humanity it seems to have gone in the can in the early 21st century. TS 18

The miracle of flesh and blood surviving in an unforgiving and truculent natural geophysical environment is solely related to the mercy, grace and power of Almighty Lord God. There truly is no other explanation. TS 18

If you think you're great, you better wait to see whether your endowed traits will evolve your fate at a later date. TS 18

The babies are the light of the world and don't ever forget it! TS 18

Having no needs is your salvation. TS 18

Thank Almighty Lord God for another day to get it right and evolve into something wonderful. TS 18

Thank Almighty Lord God for those limited souls that have the ability to embrace empathy and be motivated to show kindness and mercy to others as a result of it. TS 18

This world castigates men for being a male and a huge part of being a male is the physiological need to procreate with a woman and that driving sexual force is an innate reality of being a male; a force that the male person had nothing to do with prior to being born and assigned to be a male in this life. Therefore, what is the man supposed to be apologizing for in reference to his maleness? TS 18

The further along in this life journey I evolve, the further along I leave behind what I have known. TS 18

The blessing of ignorance is the fullness of life's pleasures that can be experienced because of it. TS 18

One great mystery and tragedy in life is the metamorphism of youthful beauty into ugly old age. TS 18

The slippery slope of wealth and its tragic end has had the ages by the balls. TS 18

People want to talk about trends when they really should be talking about all of their social relationships that are dead-ends. TS 18

Nature is willing to work with humankind to coincide but when she is abused she will become untied and people and things will fry and many people will sigh, cry or die. TS 18

I had a colleague bragging to me about having a million dollar house, then soon thereafter, he dropped dead. Did he say something wrong? TS 18

How can you do all the work and be utterly qualified, and not justifiably find a job even though you have consistently tried? TS 18

Love inverted is hate. TS 18

Showing someone mercy might just make him brand new. TS 18

All alone and needing someone to phone or to buy me an ice cream cone or to offer a helpful loan or maybe just needing to go and get stoned. TS 18

One way collective humankind is less than evolving relates to masses of educated people doing the jobs that monkeys could do. TS 18

Should the man that nearly got killed be angry with God that he nearly got killed or be thankful that he nearly got killed but didn't get killed? TS 18

When your life has devolved to a place where you have nothing left to say and all you hear is nays, then you're certainly ready to embrace a new way and some better days. TS 18

Porn and fantasy are seriously poor substitutes for social and sexual intimacy but if some folks didn't have them as coping avenues, they would surely be committing higher crimes of passion. TS 18

To not be wanted after faithfully experiencing the blood, sweat and tears to become excellent, defies logic and makes such a qualified and valiant person physically and psychologically ill. TS 18

If you're completely out of gas, I wouldn't recommend that you go to a Catholic mass; however, I would recommend that you find some passionate loving pretty damn fast! TS 18

The double-whammy is you love Tammy, but she's with Sammy. TS 18

When times are rough, don't angrily shout; be stout and gut it out! TS 18

I really don't want to achieve anything else but to be passionately loved and adored. TS 18

When the highlight of your day is taking a bath, then do the math; you're one day mercifully closer to realizing your ultimate path. TS 18

Living in a hole regardless of being on the dole, will take its toll and wreak havoc upon the soul, thereby motivating some to toke killer bowls. TS 18

Sitting around after a super typhoon on a hot cot with crotch rot while waiting for the generator to start on the dot, will motivate any man to smoke some serious pot. TS 18

For some, all alone means time to get stoned. TS 18

For some cancer patients, suffering is a bear when nobody cares and they have no hair along with some ill-advised care. TS 18

When you're suffering sick and you're at the end of your wick, don't be a prick, instead, become like a brick and learn what makes your fortitude tick. TS 18

When you have been suffering so long and resorting to doing killer bongs, why not try to become strong and live like King Kong so you can sing a new life-giving song? TS 18

You might be suffering like you have an arrow dart stuck in your heart, but don't think life's like a ranking fart, contemplate the experiential parts and commemorate them by designing some killer art. TS 18

You may be known around town as a total clown, but work to astound and then maybe, some naysayers will come around and see your worth for what it is pound for pound! TS 18

When your feet constantly itch and you think life's a bitch because you ain't filthy rich and you're ready to ditch, then it's more than likely time for you to find your healing niche. TS 18

In the end, all that matters is the power to rise you from the dead and make you an eternal blessed bed of rest because your vocational faithfulness and worthiness passed the test. TS 18

Who's going to listen to the VP whose talk is cheap and puts people to sleep because his intellect ain't too deep? TS 18

When you can no longer inspire because you've lost your passionate fire as a result of being far too tired, then maybe it's time for you to retire and find something else you can aspire to become rather than resort to just sitting on your bum? TS 18

It's true that you can actually develop and hone some talents in your life that are not natural talents and add more prolific value to your quiver of abilities. TS 18

Don't wait too late to find a loving mate because you erroneously think you don't rate or you just might end-up with a shitty fate in your addiction to masturbate. TS 18

You may not truly like yourself because you think you hold no wealth, but a closer look will find your true worthiness and beauty in the depths of your inward-self that's hidden in stealth. TS 18

When you don't confess, it just adds more duress and stress creating a life rife with strife and a plethora of women that certainly don't want to become your wife. TS 18

Before you're dead, make certain that what needs to be said is said, so nobody can say: "You didn't put to bed what needs to be said." TS 18

Inverted sexual energy somehow finds the road to death. TS 18

And how many a soul is taking a fall because nobody will empathetically call? TS 18

Those who are chronically uptight really should introspectively write rather than fly a kite or bitch about the surrounding blight. TS 18

If she won't let you close to her inner space, then maybe you're going at too fast a pace? TS 18

Some people who are perennially alone just piss and moan, when they should just be going out to consume a killer ice cream cone. TS 18

Irrational guilt will make you wilt but self-forgiveness will put you on peaceful stilts. TS 18

Anything of appetite excess may become an abscess that will become a mess and make you be less than your best so give your obsessing excess a rest. TS 18

Walk alone and forsake your smartphone and build your fortitude from a will of stone. TS 18

Boredom births forth folly that will make one a temporary jolly Charlie who in the end will just be sorry. TS 18

Rise above the useless surrounding din and no longer sin and then start accumulating some life-giving wins. TS 18

Just because you wed doesn't guarantee you'll be spiritually, socially and psychologically fed, yet it just might motivate you to make yourself or someone else dead. TS 18

Two months without electrical power would make most people cower, but the exceptional soul towers even without access to electrical power. TS 18

Those with lingering aches need a healing break or to consume a killer chocolate shake or cake. TS 18

You might be in a vocational fog rotting way like a forlorn log and living like a stray dog, but if you courageously rise-up, you can drink from the victor's cup! TS 18

You might want to pick-up the pace of your life success faster, but if so, you'll more than likely never become a master of anything but being a complete ding. TS 18

If you cannot be taught, you'll more than likely be caught in a lifestyle going for naught. TS 18

When you're a tyke, most people you like, yet as an ornery adult, you just might need a course in psych to recall that most people don't bite and can still be liked. TS 18

I once knew a guy named Truman who loved to be humid so he went-off to Tumen Bay to forever stay and now I know he certainly wasn't ever human. TS 18

If you cannot ever be led, then you're more than likely dead so enough said! TS 18

How can you say you're ok when you've never gotten laid or ever gotten seriously paid or ever had a maid? TS 18

Your greatest fear may be that nobody cares, yet that's a common irrational notion that many people share. TS 18

Your body may ache and you need to soak, take a toke, have a smoke, ingest some coke or convalesce with some soothing folks, but don't ever forsake going for broke to break your thralldom yoke. TS 18

Maybe become a fine upstart whose compelling art skillfully reaches the audience's heart and then you'll have made it on the prestige charts. TS 18

There are so many people that don't have a clue of what do in order to renew but is that anything new regardless of the few? TS 18

The person who constantly sits, watches his physical specimen go down into the pits or what you might even call the shits! TS 18

You may unfortunately be living in a humid climate that rocks and places you in a paralyzing headlock, and certainly, that has gotta be a chronic shock that's an absolute crock! TS 18

You may be obsessing about realizing more and may be feeling angrily sore, however, you have no clue as to where to find the door that leads to more and that's why people consider you a bore. TS 18

You may be piping mad that you never became a Dad and had a lad and that's more than likely factually sad, but maybe it was because you lived your life utterly bad. TS 18

You might have cast a voided vote because it was deemed a hanging chad, but that's not as bad as being a sorry-ass Dad. TS18

You might be considered very rad because you adhere to every cool fad, but having a cool Greg Brady pad is what's truly rad! TS 18

You may have started out in your life being adept at drawing with crayons and now you've evolved into the King of Sayings. TS 18

Those who are too financially tight and hang-on to this lifestyle with all of their might are really quite the sight when watching them repel the donors of light who are asking them to financially assist with helping to eradicate the community blight. TS 18

Those who are in sound mental health don't hide their wealth in stealth. TS 18

Make sure you don't cast and secure your lot in some place that so GD humid hot lest you acquire crotch rot or some other debilitating what not. TS 18

I'd rather operate some dangerous crane or drive into a water main than be vain and profane because I'm actually insane. TS 18

Being Hunky Dory has its glory but that's not usually the end of the story. TS 18

Some young poor sons go off to war carrying machine guns as they run so the victory can be won and fought no more. TS 18

Sometimes, the story of stupidity gets more intolerable and eventually the breaking point is realized because patience's strength has maxed-out. TS 18

Better sometimes not to know what's up ahead or maybe if you did know, you'd end-up dead instead. TS 18

Geez, thank Almighty Father God for the beautiful trees, the rejuvenating cool breeze and the fact that you can sneeze and get healing honey from the bees. TS 18

While there's still time, get upon your knees and thank Almighty Father God that you don't have to pay him a fee in order for him to see and show you mercy. TS 18

Slow your life down and comprehend how Almighty Father God can be found and your heartfelt thanks will become unbound. TS 18

The mind has a great tendency to pollute the heart with unbelief and in that regard, the two are like oil and water not ham and Swiss on toasted rye smothered in kraut. TS 18

A good cry cleanses away the lies and that's effectually worthy for the clarity of your eyes so you can stop asking why? TS 18

You conduct proficient business with your educated mind and the passion of your heart and soul rather than by solely wearing a suit and tie. TS 18

Forsake the takers who are the consistent fakers in reference to being movers and shakers. TS 18

In reference to your life achievements, you cannot frame them all or even completely place them in memory recall, but the fact that they have been historically realized in the annals should have you walking tall. TS 18

The wise man untapped is society being full of crap. TS18

Some people dishonorably blather their so-called knowledge and credentials and make exorbitant salaries as well, yet never have been to the heart of the matter where life issues vitally happen, and therefore, are fraudulent weaklings deserving of nothing. TS 18

Not being known and experiencing no passion is like eating USDA food rations. TS 18

The person that cannot entertain himself is at greater risk for putting a bullet in his head versus the guy who prefers to be alone. TS 18

People bloviating from their mouth like they're something, then they're suddenly dead. How weird is that? TS 18

In the final analysis of earthly living, everyone ends-up a loser. TS 18

When enduring has no viable purposeful end, then for that perceptual author, it's all over. TS 18

When hope and help don't find desperation, then desperation dies. TS 18

If God is perfect, then why are some people growing-up with crooked teeth? TS 18

How often do you have a sleep dream about the perfect girl that you're attracted to and her likewise, and then, the dream ends; however later, you dream again and she reappears and you tell her in the dream that you had a dream about her, and she tells you in the dream that she had a dream about you too! Who and where is this girl in real life? TS 18

Destruction will temporarily derail meaning and purpose and only the strong will survive it through the mercy and grace of Almighty God. TS 18

Why are Christians so zealous to believe that they have to convert remote tribes of people to their faith? If these people never hear the word of God, they are not going to be sent to hell because of their ignorance. Instead, they will be judged by other justice criteria. TS 18

The Devil's stronghold in this earthly world is ignorant, vain and unjust persons ruling over the impoverished masses. TS 18

Father God, hear the prayer of the faithful who desire to be in a community place where they can be relevant useful and healthy. Those respective communities will be better off because of it. TS 18

Father God, pray for those young single persons that long to have a family consummated in pure love and honor their precious hearts desires. TS 18

The only persons worthy of being pastors are those with a pure mind. However, how many have achieved that state of being? TS 18

The man who aspires to be pure is always in harm's way to be assailed by the Devil. Don't be deceived to believe otherwise. TS 18

Humidity and war will make a person be someone he truly is not. TS 18

The world really doesn't get any more civil simply because the collective mass of humanity doesn't even pray. TS 18

If you don't make a consistent effort to pray for other people, then why are you a good person? TS 18

Pray to Father God that the pure love that you have shown others will come back to you in full measure. TS 18

Accolades with pure motives behind them are reinvigorating like pink lemonade on a hot humid day. TS 18

Don't pray for God to save the Queen, pray for people not to be mean. TS 18

And how many useless wanderings of youth are motivated by sexual passions that realize no profitable ends? Sad indeed. TS 18

Some of what is synonymous with carrying your cross is experiencing unjustified loss. TS 18

And how wise can a young man be who is still enslaved to his "All about Me" mentality? TS 18

And how many people today are thinking: I'm so alone I just want to go home. TS 18

Some people whose lives are consumed by lust are living lives that are complete busts and that will not close-out until they develop some faith in *better yet to come* as a result of having some trust. TS 18

If you want to make a German go insane, then give him nothing to do or place him in perennial illogical situations working with moronic people void of commonsense. TS 18

Many people have been robbed because they have no job and such case by case scenarios might eventually devolve into an angry mob making their government leaders appear as slobs or even making these snobs sob. TS 18

The man who still achieves in the worst case scenarios or oppressive geophysical and social environments is your first round pick. TS 18

Pray to God that because you're not adroit that you're not sentenced to the rest of your life living in Detroit. TS 18

Someone who's a boozer might be considered a total loser or someone addicted to the sauce more than likely won't become the boss or someone who is a lush is usually in too much of a rush to ever secure some tush. TS 18

It's hard to realize spiritual and intellectual clarity living in geophysical or social environmental austerity. TS 18

Walking around all day holding a smartphone in your hand is a mental illness and multitudes are sadly afflicted with this inane disease. TS 18

Earthly life is a prison replete with much experienced derision as we ultimately wait for our debilitated and worn-out spirits, bodies and destinies to be risen. TS 18

If Jesus had his earthly physical body broken, then why do you erroneously believe that you deserve to go through this earthly life physically unscathed, yet in the meanwhile, deriving the benefits of being so-called saved? TS 18

The last page called old age certainly ain't the rage even if you're a sage. TS 18

You may be the rage while on stage, but if you're true heart's desires still remain in a cage, then that will certainly move you to eventually become enraged. TS 18

If your only point of light is hoping to dream about her again tonight, then you're certainly in quite a sorry social and psychological plight. TS 18

And what wouldn't make a man want to get stoned when he's surrounded by low-life's that just want to stare at their smartphones? TS 18

And what's more brutal and futile than working with people that have brains like noodles? TS 18

Surrounded by morons enthralled with high tech just for a paycheck would certainly explain why you might want to wring someone's neck. TS 18

Living the mundane life is a debilitating ball and chain that will drive any achievement oriented individual insane, along with its authored chronic psychological pain. TS 18

Some people resort to smoking hash once they have considered that people from their past have become like trash. TS 18

The worst concealed secret of holiness is loneliness. TS 18

Do yourself a favor every once in a while and make a run toward where you can have a ton of fun. TS 18

When your life's work has been excellently done and said, you're still going to end-up dead. TS 18

Your life upon earth is of the dirt and that in itself explains why it spiritually, physically and psychologically hurts. TS 18

Some people may want your two-sense, but you may be truly incapable because you're spent. TS 18

A man without his own home is like a dog without a bone or ice cream without a cone or a castle without stone or a beauty without a comb or a teen without a smartphone or the Air Force without a drone or a telephone without a tone or a business-start-up without a loan and finally, someone who probably needs to get freaking stoned! TS 18

Basking in self-adulation and fame is pretty lame and actually quite the shame. TS 18

American Christianity is impotent as a transforming faith because of its mass idolatry of adherents whose hearts are half-in and half-out. TS 18

All this work and no reward so where is the Lord? See the prodigal son story and the second son who came in from the field. TS 18

They say, if you long-term suffer it makes you rougher and tougher, but I will say, it will primarily set you down on your duffer! TS 18

At any time, nature will eat-up humankind so don't be arrogantly blind and take no mind or you'll be in a serious bind when nature comes calling upon you acting very unkind. TS 18

Having nothing left to do and having nobody to drop by to say, "Hi" is like shit on rye. TS 18

The primary story of life upon earth for humanity is about suffering. TS 18

And how many people deceivingly believed that they would receive their rewarded lot on the dot, and instead, they just found out in the end, it was all for not? TS 18

Greed in the heart is like a ranking fart and those who are in bondage to it aren't very smart. TS 18

Two things in life that are very fine are a pleasurable dine and the number 69. TS 18

How can you ever win when you're entrenched in willful sin? TS 18

Think of how many people will never be met by you because your so-called beliefs are set and you stupidly don't want them upset? TS 18

Truthfully, there are far too many oppressive ruthless fools in rule that need to either go to school, be drowned in a pool or fall upon a sharpened tool. TS 18

And after the wealthy man dies, he now gets to be buried in a suit and tie; and although he wasn't anyone's favorite guy and more than likely nobody's going to cry, most people won't be shy about going to his post-burial luncheon to eat some of his grandma's favorite apple pie as they feign their sorry goodbyes. TS 18

I'd rather live on the moon or in a closet room than suffer through the aftermath of a super typhoon in June. TS 18

Until you're relegated to Stone Age living, what is it that you're saying you know? TS 18

Some people would rather get lost on the Appalachian Trail than get a root canal and wail after the procedure fails. TS 18

A cataclysmic event might put your life in a dent or make you see that your current life goals are utterly spent, on hold or need to be subjected to remold. TS 18

Some people would rather be living in the austere cold than to be totally told. TS 18

Your Thanksgiving Dinner ain't going to last so why instead don't you fast? TS 18

I once knew a guy named Jack who was seriously addicted to Crack and loved eating Big Macs; yet both lifestyle choices were associated with him having a serious heart attack which ultimately put him on his back which later devolved him into living in a shack; and ever since, his life has been out-of-whack and these are no lies but just the facts about Jack. TS 18

There isn't any place to go on this earth now where you can procure lasting peace and security and that's a certainty. TS 18

The smartphone has ushered in mass frivolity and secured its presence to new heightened levels – guaranteeing more brain dead, irrelevant and powerless deceived masses of souls. TS 18

My life has devolved into being Paul in jail in Rome and me just waiting to die now because the race has been run and the mission purpose is done. TS 18

When you completely realize this physical body is your burden and your enemy, now you're ready to die in peace. TS 18

Unfortunately, you cannot gain consistent perceptual clarity without going through austerity and that's why so many stupid decisions are made over and over again. TS 18

Some people will be going to the CEM today who aren't prepared to go and their material things they worshipped during this earthly life will not be in tow. TS 18

America is the home of the scam, the sham and the utter shame and that truly is the name of the game in a place replete with personal idolatry that's so lame. TS 18

Unfortunately, the people who are in power with the final say, are usually the ones who never pray. TS 18

And how many people every day are falling upon their sword who have never even sought the Lord? TS 18

Don't confuse the Devil's hatred for humanity with God's chastisement. TS 18

Nothing to do after a super typhoon would turn any sane man into a loon. TS 18

I believe Almighty God has damned Saipan. TS 18

The ozone's depleting and procuring stupid fame is fleeting. TS 18

The spiritual bankruptcy of your heart is like a ranking fart. TS 18

The incessant debilitating humid heat of Saipan utterly rocks, yet it's such a crock and it would make any man not give a damn about any so-called Godly plan. TS 18

There is a only a very tiny population of people upon this earth that have the self-discipline to still create amidst being assailed by absolute hate, yet they are truly the cadre of people that should rule over the indolent sheeples. TS 18

The fortitude power of Almighty Lord God knows no end, and therefore, the needy man needs to find a way to tap into it in order to not only survive, but to become productive in the worst of times. TS 18

You may be experiencing physical, social or psychological dread, but be of good cheer and consider how many people who have already come and gone upon this earth that are already dead. TS 18

Pray to God that he can transform your life from a person that cowers into a tower of power. TS 18

Pray that someday you can live to joyfully sing in reference to the end of the reign of the moronic dings. TS 18

Those persons who can only talk, don't know the price of the lonely walk and assuredly always cowardly balk when asked to take that courageous walk. TS 18

Saipan: Hell upon earth with very little mirth. TS 18

The Devil's going to take what he's going to take and let's see if you have what it takes to circumvent his efforts to take what he's going to take. TS 18

There's no utility in futility. TS 18

A natural disaster will bring forth visually the totality of losers in a community for all to see. TS 18

Be of good cheer and have no fear, for if you're an iconoclast then you're in good company because Jesus was an iconoclast too! TS 18

You may be eating multiple dinners and be considered a gluttonous sinner even though you actually are a winner; however, you surely will not be getting any thinner! TS 18

Inevitably, if the wise man is truly wise then he will be cast out and unable to travel about, and that's not because he has gout, it's because the surrounding hateful world is entrenched in doubt. TS 18

As the billows of darkness roll and take their toll, many people lose their soul. TS 18

If you're a bitcher, it might make you temporarily richer, but no one will lie for you at your funeral. TS 18

Good therapy should help people remember what they're trying to forget so their heart healing can be met. TS 18

The person who can take on fear has the fighting heart of a bear even though he initially may be unaware or not even care that people think he is courageous to take on his fears. TS 18

And how many loser friends from your past have forsaken you out of shame and isn't that freaking lame? TS 18

In the time of your deep darkness, find your art. TS 18

Maybe lust is being confused with the desire to apprehend pure love? TS 18

A man knows who his lass is. TS 18

The teacher without a mentee is the father without the son. TS 18

How could anyone actually think that living without being touched is good? TS 18

You probably better have something beautiful to show for your earthly time or your final judgment ain't going to be so fine. TS 18

Your secured private living space keeps you physically and psychologically healthy. TS 18

The generation change starts with the neonates. TS 18

Donald Kuciewski was a fine example of a man that like to tinker with a solid buzz on. TS 18

Warren Brock was the best bread man ever! Hands down! TS 18

Some people's glory is their public life yet their *bipolar other life* is full of strife. TS 18

The longer the Lord waits for retaliation, the greater the ass-beating to come. TS 18

For so many mid-life people it's about no more love. TS 18

The Vatican is the epitomy of idolatry and no one seems to care. TS 18

Masses of Cambodian people are dirt road poor but just as vital too! TS 18

The Koreans love success and Seoul is their crowning jewel. TS 18

Up in the North Tower looking down at the blanket of smog snaking through the valley over vast Seoul and all I could say was "Oh no, poor Seoul." TS 18

If you can satisfy the need then you don't have to continue to feed and just maybe you can lead. TS 18

And what am I predominantly contending with but people that don't know anything. TS 18

Too much access takes away the mystique so keep them away when necessary. TS 18

Too much access takes away the mystique and that means less power. TS 18

Your liquid capital burns as the world turns with minimal lasting returns. TS 18

Sometimes, when there's nothing to do it's good to think about people's lives who have already been through. TS 18

What I remember about Paul Ivancic was he was always trying to get a chick because he had no chick. TS 18

Frank Ivancic's legacy was he was a prick married to an obsequious chick. TS 18

What I remember about Uncle John was he was a Don. TS 18

Yet, Uncle Dave was a fav because he and Aunt Veronica were completely the rave. TS 18

And Uncle Footie loved his sticks but he had a lot of versatile blue collar tricks and there wasn't anything he couldn't fix. TS 18

And Lenny Batiak had a stern face that could give any Beatnik a heart attack. TS 18

And how many Catholics think they're going to purgatory or heaven just because they're Catholics? TS 18

What I remember about Uncle Bill was his crooked front teeth looked pretty ill and I know I wasn't in his will. TS 18

The things I remember about my Great Uncle Nick was that he had quite the outstanding memory and wit and I never saw him throw a fit. TS 18

What I remember about Uncle Larry was his wife was always giving him crap when all he wanted to do was take a nap. TS 18

The thing I remember about my Aunt Rose was her laid back manner never required you to be on your toes and she did have quite the big nose. TS 18

What I remember about my Step Grandpa Joe was he had a huge nose and because he was always saying, "For Crying Out Loud," I assumed he thought much of life blows! TS 18

The thing I remember about Grandma most was her killer tasty lasagna was something worthy of a serious boast! TS 18

What I remember about my Cousin Barbara's husband Tom was he was always on leave from Viet-Nom (Nam). TS 18

What I remember about my friend Matt was he never took any crap and that he was a 38-year-old virgin and that wasn't something he wanted to be. TS 18

The addict tries so very hard to repeat the best highs he's had so that he can be very much glad, but the long-term ramifications for him are usually pretty bad and that's pretty sad. TS 18

I remember Mr. Moeller who always looked like he was stuck in the late fifties with his *rolled cuffed at the bottom* dungarees and Brylcreem hair that would give any hot chick a mighty scare. TS 18

I remember Mrs. Sitek who would spy on me through her front window and although that would normally make any young guy a wreck, for me it was no big spectacle because I knew she was playing with a half a deck; so hell, what could I expect from someone like Mrs. Sitek? TS 18

Running people around and dumbing them down will make any plans made go south into the ground. TS 18

The micro world of nature is just waiting to take over. TS 18

I'm tired of leading because my heart ain't bleeding. TS 18

When the loneliness takes over and nothing can take it away, then you're in a bad-off way. TS 18

When we die, are we going to be in a place where we're smiling all the time? TS 18

Dragging our bodies along for the earthly ride is what ultimately makes the mind fried. TS 18

A disaster will cleanse fantasy from your heart and hopefully give you a new start lest you remain a disobedient Godless retart. TS 18

Life without a passionate kiss is quite the diss that nobody would wish. TS 18

So many people are piss poor that they cannot even find the door to realize something greater more and hence some women become whores and some dudes rob stores and some people down cases of Coors. TS 18

A person's mind can be dark but his art can still be on the mark and off the charts. TS 18

Nothing left to do means maybe going to Timbuktu with a girl named Sue to realize something new. TS 18

And truly, how much of your life has been a waste of time not worthy of a dime and shouldn't that be considered a felonious crime especially if it has all gone down in your prime? TS 18

It's all for the mouth and because of the mouth that people's lives inevitably go south. TS 18

I should have stayed in Tonawanda and married Rhonda. TS 18

What makes life utterly meaningless on earth is the fact that there has been and currently is no pervasive justice administered toward healing mass people's lives and this is documented through a painstaking study of human history. In truth, multitudes suffering throughout history is synonymous with zero justice being implemented upon their behalf. And who can refute this fact and in the meanwhile, defend the goodness and mercy of God in reference to this topical area of analysis? TS 18

The generation after you and after that, forgets you and everything you knew and that's that! TS 18

Irrational guilt and humidity are a volatile combination for instigating physical illness and definitely would not be compared as going to together well like spaghetti and meatballs in red sauce. TS 18

The man that can practice patience in pervasive and hot humid conditions is a near God. TS 18

Some people may actually hide from you because they don't want their face to confide to you that they love you. TS 18

And where does the pure and pristine energy that motivates the little child's feet go off to? TS 18

Your arduous journeying will not stop until you make a commitment to learning what you need to know without capitulating those responsibilities in deference to your cope-out philosophy *that everything blows*. TS 18

If your body's bleeding then maybe your patience is receding. TS 18

If you're a social creep then you're headed for the neap where people you oppressed will want to take a peep at you. TS 18

Without love lust is dead. TS 18

Your fatigue is related to you being *out-of-your-league.* TS 18

And what do the molecules of anger, guilt and fear look like? TS 18

The son of man having no place to lay his head is heartbreaking. TS 18

Almighty God will never allow the Devil to exceed the laws of nature when he unleashes destruction – even though much incomprehensible damage will ensue. See typhoons, cyclones, hurricanes, tornados, tsunamis, earthquakes for details. TS 18

Today, most women don't want a real man like Steve McQueen or Paul Newman. TS 18

Dying is bad enough, but to be dying in a place where you're not wanted and don't want to be, isn't like sharing a loving and merciful cup of tea. TS 18

The riffraff come out of the jungle when the Fed is offering free giveaways so as to be fed in order to help them from being dead. TS 18

How can it be that you never have anything to say about any given day? TS 18

Some people come-out of the woodwork and then after their confession, they go back into the woodwork. Ala Gary Hagler. TS 18

The shepherd's gig is 24 hours 7 days. TS 18

Maybe because you are *yourself* that's why you have little wealth, no help and shitty health? TS 18

The purity of the child's voice heals. TS 18

Ignorance and decision-making are not charbroiled hot dogs with dill relish, mustard and onions on a warm toasted bun. TS 18

Use your time wisely and in doing so, make certain that you're planning some pleasure for yourself too! TS 18

You would think you'd want to know, but instead, you choose to be a no-show and the consequence is you remain imprisoned living real low with your kid in tow. TS 18

Finding love through an *Act of God* is God doing you a big-time favor that has nothing to do with your labor in order to gain favor; so therefore, without waver, partake and savor because she is a saver. TS 18

A 65-year-old guy that can barely walk waiting around for another paycheck is a pretty sad sight to lay eyes upon. TS 18

You could be tragically economically poor or be considered spiritually poor, and likewise as a consequence, either rob a store or be enslaved to your religion and thereby not be experiencing living anymore. Nevertheless, in both of these case scenarios where the persons are poor, they are both in dire need to be shown the door to something greater more. TS 18

If you do what you think is right and it was really wrong, then God will maybe forgive you, but your penalty that cannot be amended is the cost of your time forever lost doing the wrong thing. TS 18

Guilt inhibits healing from being realized and keeps debilitating addictions rockin and rolling. TS 18

Those people in this world that have a clue are extraordinarily very few and those multitudes who are utterly lost with their lives in the loo is absolutely nothing new. TS 18

Guys, when your life is rife with strife, then it's time for you to get a new life or maybe it means that it's time for you to find a beautiful compassionate wife? TS 18

Carrying the cross always entails loss, but maybe these experiences qualify you to be the boss? TS 18

If you're a grown man then you need to get-off from sitting on your hands and make a stand to get your own land and rescue your life out of the quicksand. TS 18

The astute mind logically considers it not unwise to be kind to the people who are the feeble sheeples. TS 18

Chasing after earthly mammon your entire life leads to an eternal famine with quite the nasty bite! TS 18

No justice upon earth has quite the factual evidence of girth along with little mirth. TS 18

If weeks after a super typhoon you're dreaming about the generator, then most certainly you are wired. TS 18

In the final analysis as Solomon said, the writing of many books is a wearisome endless task, but it's probably better than being a crook. TS 18

The man that chronically lies dishonors himself and his professed religion. TS 18

How can someone be a Taoist, Buddhist and Jew all at the same time, and yet, still not have a clue of what to do? TS 18

The quest for pure love that ends in death certainly isn't the fairy tale ending we desire to hear about or see; however, pray to Almighty God that you can peaceable say, "I'm glad this story isn't about me." TS 18

Peripheral living doesn't give-out any first-place ribbons. TS 18

The comfortable easy life is great, but in eternal time it becomes obscured and faint. TS 18

So much talent goes by the waste side because there is no communication about those people who have talent and thereby no connected relationships for those identified with talent. Therefore, there are no impending sponsorships or mentorships toward the beginning, middle and end for such talented individuals in their quest to achieve excellence in any given field. TS 18

The man with clarity, even after major upset, is the Prez. TS 18

My door's open and she won't come to visit because she wants to keep all the power; yet, that really is only obscuring her true acts of cowardice. TS 18

For those who lived their entire life and didn't procreate – while in the meanwhile - society has said they don't really rate - I say, don't die in hate, but try to realize a clean slate so you will die in a peaceable state. TS 18

Flesh and blood and eroding away like crud and then it's out with a thud! TS 18

Amassing and reviewing your material artifacts is not idolatry when it's done for comprehending the meaning of your legacy and understanding how it was achieved. TS 18

The curse of those desires of the flesh is that those desires are never satisfied - hence a primary origin for explaining addictions or shipwrecked lives. TS 18

Don't blow your fuse and verbally or physically abuse or you might just be making the news. TS 18

For the good and the bad and what has been pretty sad or has made you totally mad, some unfortunately will always remember not having a Dad and that's what has really made it for them all extraordinarily rad! TS 18

For once in your life, do the right thing and lift someone up. TS 18

For some people, an encouraging word might fuel them for months so they can achieve even more good. TS 18

I know a lot of Roman Catholic people who have faithfully went to mass but it didn't prevent a super typhoon from giving them a pass and handing them their ass. TS 18

When Almighty God destroys his own edifices of worship what does that mean? TS 18

Good and faithful friends touching base in order to review your case or just to see your face regardless of your race never goes to waste and is like a fine wine with a lasting - pleasurable taste. TS 18

Twenty years ago, I remember these local leaders in the church where I attended that said they were going to pray every Tuesday night at the altar; I think the blowhards pulled it off one time and quit! Some true role models in faith and perseverance. Classic. TS 18

How can you have faith when your heart is idolatry? TS 18

The only thing I can remember about American Christianity is what a sham it was. TS 18

When the suffering comes to your home and physical body, now you're going to be singing a new song – so what does that say about the strength and accuracy of what you believed all along in reference to the goodness of God? TS 18

The sacrifice of a human life to reach a goal is never acceptable – especially if you're the one being selected to be sacrificed. TS 18

At 55 years-old – what I remember most was making the acquaintance with Ibuprofen. TS 18

Pain will chase away the so-called faithful. TS 18

God kicking your ass when you're down is not love. TS 18

Why would a counseling agency call itself: Good Intention Counseling? What the hell other kind of intention is the consumer supposed to expect? Asinine. TS 18

I once knew a girl named Dawn who never had any man fawn over her. However, she had a chance to go to France to meet a man named Shawn, yet unfortunately, she decided to stay back and lived the rest of her life in total lack as a barren old maid because she couldn't be sold to break her dysfunctional lifestyle mold. Sad indeed and quite the tragedy! TS 18

In reference to love and justice being administered, history *in major league baseball season terms* is a 70-92. TS 18

Some people's social life is as silent as being in the grave or in a deep abandoned mining cave, yet such souls living in such debasement are actually quite brave. TS 18

I don't want accolades I just want a maid. TS 18

Access to no utilities transforms the genteel man into a sad impotent man. TS 18

Without access to consistent novel imagery or themes, porn loses its addictive power. TS 18

Maybe someday, someone will waken-up from the dead and remember you and help you with an opportunity to become socially and vocationally unglued and completely brand new. TS 18

And what's the epitomy of hate but someone struggling for his last living breaths while his family looks on as this atrocity unfolds? TS 18

Cruel and unusual punishment is no pickle on the *last meal* cheeseburger. TS 18

And it would do the world some serious good to sentence these vain and ignorant government and corporate leaders to two to five years without access to any utilities. TS 18

Maybe the sack upon Santa's back has something for you in reference to what you lack or maybe the Wizard of Oz's black bag has something to keep away the fags dressed in drag? TS 18

Injustices steal multiple outcomes to be and such people authoring such denied outcomes are bums. TS 18

Hopefully, the home the Lord is preparing for you isn't on skid row in Manila. TS 18

If you die in a socially-imposed prison, then maybe he really was never risen? TS 18

I don't want to be hot and I don't want to be cold, I just want to be in 72 degrees with a slight breeze. TS 18

A lot of the demons in this earthly world are residing on remote islands in ocean locations. TS 18

The problem with natural disasters isn't just the immediate destruction from the event itself, but the residual consequences such as disease development that debilitates or kills people later on. TS 18

If you're living with a dipshit or twit who may potentially flip, maybe you need to split. TS 18

Today, I saw the craziest event. I saw a middle-aged Filipino dude get out of his car and smile with no front teeth in his mouth; he then proceeded to take out his comb from his back pants pocket in order to comb over the bald spot on his head. Dude! Does it really matter to comb over the bald spot on your head when you have no front teeth in your mouth? TS 18

If you're dying on the side of the road it's not likely the riff raff passing by will take you out of the cold; however, if someone does stop to consider your plight, it might just be to get you sold. TS 18

It's come to my perceptual forefront that all of the years of doing the so-called right thing didn't really help me and didn't really help anyone else. TS 18

The surface will certainly tell us a little about what's going-on below, but we can never entirely know when the Yellowstone Caldera region is going to blow and put an end to the USA show! TS 18

Even though I'm living in a worst case scenario now, it has not changed my life philosophy of not worrying about what tomorrow may bring that I have no control over. TS 18

Some people live their entire lives with little cash and thereby they are perceived by many others as trash suffering great abash. TS 18

Truthfully, not many people have a desire to abnegate their fantasy-based driven activities in order to stop masturbating. TS 18

If love is the fulfillment of the law, then how is love ever bad or corrupt? Think this through and consider where it applies? TS 18

Claiming ownership of land and natural resources is laughable; no man owns nature; if anything, nature owns man and geophysical realities far outlive his vain self. TS 18

Chasing and worshipping mammon is a waste of time and ends in eternal famine. TS 18

The people who are getting their fleshly needs met all of the time are probably actually worshipping the Devil and they think they're worshipping Christ. In truth, the Holy Spirit doesn't work to primarily meet your physical desires and needs 24/7 because a phenomena called austerity is the purifier. Total deception to believe otherwise. TS 18

I didn't abandon God he abandon me. TS 18

It could be that our death obliterates any memories we have of our earthly life and personal identity. TS 18

And what serves as the diabolical lid as we live is that we cannot completely remember everything that we have did. TS 18

If a pure heart cannot deliver the goods, then where else can you start? TS 18

Who can carry the cross of misery in all purity? No one I know of that's for sure. TS 18

The only way the man who is vain can stop being vain is to experience some serious pain. TS 18

It's time for a baby to minister to my soul lest the living train wreck I'm upon takes its toll. TS 18

The man that is perceived of as so-called less that shows you mercy and compassion truly is your master. TS 18

Some people may be erroneously thinking they need another job to change their life, when maybe it's really time for them to leave this earth? TS 18

When your physical strength is gone, how can you have any patience? TS 18

The walk of no pleasure is like being in a barren desert or in bad weather and it certainly is not a psychological feather. TS 18

Some of our emotions are birthed into existence by vain notions and we really need a special potion or lotion to put them out of motion. TS 18

Only the resurrection power of Christ can prevail; all else will surely fail. TS 18

Real life in the real world is the best living. TS 18

It's unfortunate that a primarily historical and contemporary human race thinks it can define God – when if the common held belief by these people is that God is infinite – then how comprehensively can they truly define such an infinite God with their finite minds? TS 18

Living in the world that shouldn't be is listening to noise that shouldn't be; paying exorbitant tax and other related life fees; never being able to buy yet always having to rent or lease; wondering whether he is a she or a he?; always having to take a pee; being around mindless losers who have a mentality of: "It's all about Me;" always losing your car keys; being surrounded by ignorant fools who cannot see, and never finding a place where someone will just leave you to be. TS 18

It's the majority of people who cannot stand to think and be alone that are addicted to their smartphones so when the laws of electricity change, they will be the ones who will suffer the greatest psychological pain and maybe even become deranged. TS 18

Why should you care if someone twenty years younger than you doesn't respect you? He will soon enough be getting his series of ass-beatings to comprehend what it's like to be in your shoes. TS 18

Time bears out the truth of all things and that's why wanting to become a preacher is as dumb as you can be. TS 18

Preaching is for those ignorant individuals who haven't had much extensive life experience, and they get away with their pompous blathering's by preaching to people dumber than themselves. TS 18

The man that welcomes hardship is a dipshit and eventually he'll live to see it sink his ship. TS 18

If someone isn't consistently working to make your life more comfortable or productive, then they're probably not your friend. TS 18

When you have sucked the pleasures out-of-life, then your personal chaos may now begin to abound and astound! TS 18

Unfortunately, many of the great artifacts of our biographical life will make curbside due to ignorance and apathy. TS 18

You don't sit in a place of hellish austerity for ten years and believe Almighty God loves you unless you're truly mentally ill. TS 18

Hedonism and its relentless will, will eventually kill. TS 18

A super typhoon is like a kick in the teeth or a kick in the balls, but one thing for sure, everyone will fall! TS 18

I don't feel guilty about a requisite physiological need unless it's related to hurting someone because of the deed. TS 18

You may be a bitcher, but if you're still here, you're more than likely a bear! TS 18

What does it mean when your former pastor left the ministry to sell tools for a living? TS 18

Being poor, not good enough and not knowing enough ain't getting you the girl you want. TS 18

Let me just hug the little babies for the rest of my life and I'm all set until this party's over. TS 18

There are so many people in the USA that have their head-up their ass and that factually is associated with the demise of the nation. TS 18

Having your head-up your ass can be operationally defined in behaviorally specific terms so don't say it ain't so as an endemic societal condition. TS 18

Getting a little high on and feeling a little cool air is a fine respite and changes misery into comfort for a thankful NY number of minutes. TS 18

Nature is primary over man all of the time; and until you experience it – you truly know nothing. TS 18

I wouldn't want to have my ass handed to me because it was overdue – that would be death. TS 18

Having a baby in your loving arms and knowing all is right with the world is a fine place to be. TS 18

Look in the baby's eyes and he will learn. TS 18

I've had enough of academia and these dumb-ass people who are sitting and shitting in it and running these institutions of higher education into the ground. TS 18

The middle-aged man knows it's over for him when the young beautiful girl comes over to say hi, but soon enough she is saying, "I gotta say goodbye." TS 18

The hate in this world is like an insurmountable fortress and only Almighty Lord God can help you overcome it. TS 18

The larger issues of life that imprison you that you're ignorant of, you are truly powerless over. TS 18

And how many of you have done the Gene Hackman (Reverend Scott) thing? See his last scene in the Poseidon Adventure. TS 18

Idolatry to the things of this world is the bottom of the barrel. TS 18

The hateful and jealous spirit cannot give but that's what makes it continue to live. TS 18

I still remember the old man who donated all his old dirty sneakers and some other useless trinkets to my agency in the early 21st century. Surely, he must be dead now and I'm certain the sneakers and trinkets are rotting away in some place of useless utility. TS 18

Everybody in Saipan has tuberculosis; that's a given and that deserves the world health organization's (WHO) first place blue ribbon! TS 18

Whatever happened to Walter Barnes and his son who kicked ass operating the 3 and 1 bucket? TS 18

And what happened to the other old NC hillbilly without the 3 and 1 bucket who said there was never a tree he couldn't knock down with his dozer, yet the job he was interviewing for was to remove stumps and save the trees. TS 18

If treated bad enough for long enough, anyone can become mentally ill. TS 18

Teaching people to have faith about a future unknown that actually could turn out to be utterly horribly thrown is kind of irresponsible and/or hateful don't you think? TS 18

Part of being amidst the living dead is you exist – but no one talks to you; no one visits you; no one knows you or your existence is unknown. TS 18

The Internet is just a redundant version of the Encyclopedia Britannica with sound. TS 18

It's amazing what a brilliant teacher can communicate with just a piece of chalk and a chalkboard or a dry erase marker and dry erase board. TS 18

In most cases, the prophet's going to die and no one is going to help him. TS 18

If anything has any irrefutable truth it's empiricism – especially the fact that whatever currently remains a constant can change at any time as documented from the past. TS 18

There's the magnificent beauty of the created giraffe and the absolute ugliness of the socially-constructed riff raff who comprise a large part of the global map. TS 18

Masses of people dying and no one crying primes the world for an impending frying. TS 18

An opportunity created especially for you by the Lord keeps you from falling upon your sword. TS 18

Governing: The folly of humankind. TS 18

The earthly community has devolved into a miserable place and the greedy people's stronghold needs some serious mace in the face! TS 18

The national government's primary role is to protect its border and the communities within those borders should take care of each other. TS 18

Deflate the greed and now see well-being replenished with health and hope to meet the needs. TS 18

Sit in your *la la land* while I sit in my jail, and hey, maybe we can become pals? TS 18

And Jesus Christ knows of no joy associated with no reward for a job well done. TS 18

And think of those many souls that are presented before you every day for something, and then ask, what did I add in for them during the meanwhile? TS 18

The first behavioral step a person in chronic pain should implement is relieving his guilt. TS 18

You can be in such austerity that you lose yourself in the coping. TS 18

Now I know why Jesus would sometimes leave the crowd of needy people. TS 18

People bitch about parents using a belt on their children; however, life on earth is the real ass-beating. TS 18

Don't be afraid to show your beautiful self. TS 18

Think about someone you knew well that is now dead and stop and ask yourself, where is he or she right now? TS 18

The purer the motive, the greater the clarity of truth to guide you. TS 18

The two spirits – good versus evil – war against each other to gain control of the heart and mind of the individual; hence, the bipolar sagacity that defines and explains the human condition. TS 18

The "Let's make you our King" spirit that Jesus contended with still exists in the world today thereby shipwrecking many good intended purposes. TS 18

The best instructor can practically apply what he is teaching and demonstrate that information to be behaviorally modeled if needed. TS 18

If I am a scholar and nobody can learn anything from me – then I might soon be working at McDonald's with nobody giving me a holler. TS 18

Any historian knows that the geo-physical world has its own will and it imposes it upon social life all of the time – including in some ways that are disastrous. TS 18

Russian missiles will never kill us but McRib's might. TS 18

In 2018, I was baptized as a genuine Pacific Island man by going 42 days (six weeks) without access to 24 hour utilities; suffering an MRSA staph infection on my back for five weeks and losing 3 lower bottom teeth while experiencing the excruciating pain that goes along with that experience – such as being unable to bite into a sandwich or any food item for a year. TS 18

Consistently travelling by plane is not an option for me now as I enter into my late fifties and for many like me experiencing this fact, our vocational options are truly limited. Moreover, more than likely, we will need to establish a viable way to make a living until retirement in a home base location with little or no itinerant options. TS 18

My final grade for my six week super typhoon Yutu boot camp was a 72% or C minus. I exemplified outstanding courage, fortitude, adaptability, focus and physical stamina, along with super artistic and intellectual productivity, yet it was marred by too much hate and bitching. TS 18

And thank Almighty Lord God today for the pleasure of taste and all of its diverse offerings! TS 18

I disqualified myself from becoming a pastor years ago, yet then again, that's not accurately relevant because no one is truly qualified to hold such a position anyhow unless they're blind to their own immoral conditions. TS 18

The double-whammy with Tammy is she is still dealing with her ex named Sammy and she already has her own family. TS 18

Not being able to flush a toilet properly for 42 days might not faze some people and others would be amazed, and some might think it part of a hazing or a new craze, while finally, some might just accept it as a sign of the last days. TS 18

It looks like Ms. Pi was punched in the side of her right eye and I wonder why she stays with this guy when she should be leaving this town and telling this clown goodbye! TS 18

21st century Christianity in the USA has as its poison – too much comfort – thereby truly not being able to evolve into a level of holiness that Christ leads believers toward. TS 18

It's very difficult to respect people that know very little about suffering and have inherited opportunity and wealth despite their limited talents and skills. TS 18

And what's most terrible for some people is not having any family to count upon. TS 18

I'm in a social prison, but at least the Apostle Paul had dedicated visitors. TS 18

The problem with being a young adult with a lot of talents is accurately knowing the best path to choose vocationally that you believe in – especially in reference to it feeling and being right. TS 18

The most effective antibiotics are:

1. Passionate love.

2. Truth.

3. Zero guilt.

4. Faith.

5. Vocational Purpose.

6. Loving Encouragement.

7. Confession.

8. Prayer.

9. Having Access to an Empathetic Listener.

10. Hope.

11. Intercessory Helping or Prayer. TS 18

Honestly, how many antibiotic farts can a man blow? TS 18

In the end, the only thing that matters is what Almighty God thinks of you because he's the only one that has access to all of the truthful facts about you. TS 18

Love can sustain borders and love can transcend borders. TS 18

The solidifying key to any intimate relationship is vulnerabilities exposed. TS 18

Lying can be complicated. TS 18

In the world that should be, someone who values your personhood and your talents is alongside of you for the ride – encouraging and strengthening you so the destiny of your actualized self and calling might be fulfilled. Unfortunately however, we don't live in the world that should be we live in the world that is, and that's why the majority of us cannot take care of our life biz. TS 18

To believe in the depth of your soul that everything you have achieved through perseverance was for nothing is the highest level of heartbreak. TS 18

It's nice that Jesus loves you, but you still have to place bread in your mouth and the challenge for the truly faithful that know the real deal is the majority of the world that surrounds you won't afford you opportunities to get your bread. TS 18

Having nothing to do of any substantial relevant utility will serve to unglue most but the exceptional few. TS 18

Dead-end lies motivate extra-love affairs because the mind and physical body gets bored to tears quite quickly. TS 18

How much time and energy is wasted in each person's life is truly fascinating. TS 18

The world's hate is powerful and much of it remains in place in order to keep comfort and leisure in a status quo position as multitudes suffer because of this. TS 18

Until you've had someone dig out of the ground and steal the 7 foot tall Frazier Fir Christmas tree you planted in your front yard (when it was only 3 foot tall) then what the hell is it that you say you know and believe in? TS 18

Don't be so cocky because someone might take the generator of your life away at any time. TS 18

The gamut of emotions that you experience after living through a natural disaster that almost killed you and destroyed your home and surrounding community cannot be completely understood because the lexicon has no words to give meaning to the emotions related to this experience. TS 18

From the typhoon, I inherited a scar on the palm of my right hand and a gash on my right lower side and a scar in the middle of my left foot. For me, it's not beginning to look like Christmas, it's beginning to look like Jesus and Gethsemane. TS 18

The state of US healthcare is so deplorable just because you pay handsomely for zero quality care. For instance, the other day, a stupid doctor tells me it's ok to take two different antibiotics at the same time. Dude, you don't even know the results of the culture of the bacteria I am fighting right now and you're recommending for me to take two antibiotics at the same time that might not even be applicable to the results of a lab culture that's not yet determined? Idiocy! Take that fucking white coat off – this ain't Halloween! TS 18

Billions of profits made from greed, waste, aggrandizement and incompetence; and yes, there are losers indeed as a consequence. TS 18

If you're at the end of your life and there is much to show for a life that has produced helping, love, learning and achievements, then you're in a very thankful place indeed. TS 18

Ask Jesus to help you with the strength that he provides and he will faithfully help you. TS 18

To be surrounded by people that won't give-up love because of the social construction of norms relates to the question: how much of a misery is that? TS 18

I'm on the unthinkable trail of hardship now and I'm falling down all of the time and it's not a pretty sight to behold as I fear I might fold. TS 18

Jesus is the only MD you'll ever need. TS 18

What do you know about this earthly life until you've taken the heartbreak for Almighty God's sake? TS 18

Thank the Almighty Father God for the life of bountiful supply that he has historically provided in reference to your physical and psychological health, along with opportunities for love, shelter, food, friends, and opportunities for vocational growth and expression. TS 18

Let's go play church and see if we can find some people in the lurch. TS 18

Don't ask me if I need help and then offer me zero help. That's the highest level of hate you can show me. TS 18

If you want to drain immaturity and impurities of the heart, then you bring a disaster to derail the life party gravy train. TS 18

And how many have steadily amassed yet have been given a free pass in reference to loss and a spanking on the ass? TS 18

Be sober and comprehend that somewhere along the line your life party is going to end so make sure you're getting your soul on the mend before it does come to a crashing end! TS 18

I wouldn't mind having a couple of margaritas with Florita! TS 18

Healthcare: Paying moronic people money to give you ignorant advice in a short-shrifted social interactive context. TS 18

Hearing bad news at the wrong time is a serious fine imposed and who knows what soul could truly stay composed or might unravel and become exposed? TS 18

Some of these people fulfilling their so-called American Dream truly aren't even qualified to be holding the positions of remuneration they possess and that's the sham and shame of their lives and the American Dream itself! TS 18

The great leveler is everybody takes an undignified shit so don't think you're the shit when you're really a piece of shit that's still taking shits! TS 18

Truly, life on earth is sitting on death row. TS 18

Youth passes away and you get ugly, fat and blubbery and then, it's all social entrenched drudgery. TS 18

Enjoy it while you can assholes, because your pretty little houses are going to fall like a deck of cards and you'll be wearing thread bares when your life judgment is finally passed and you failed with a final grade of F+. Well done. TS 18

And don't forget that you have some chicks acting all great who are on their damn way that you're never going to get to lay because they'd rather proudly announce they're gay, thereby keeping all legitimate male suitors at bay. TS 18

Life upon earth is the only show in town you clown so make it count. TS 18

"You can take your money honey and shove it up your ass!" exclaimed the dummy. TS 18

How can health be realized and maintained when there is no justice in the land? TS 18

Beware: Antibiotics will tear you a new colon asshole bro. TS 18

Just waiting to die as an old man and sitting around drooling – now who the hell are you fooling thinking you can still do some dueling and ruling when what's truly happening to you is just plain grueling? TS 18

So many people are so alone waiting for a bone and that's why in the meanwhile, they're getting stoned. TS 18

The prudent, wise or productive people versus the impetuous, foolish or indolent people live their lives, but all end with a last breath – and then – death. So where is the justice in that same type of conclusion *when the one size fits all ending* rules over humanity regardless of how anyone has lived? TS 18

Whether you're wise, productive, foolish or indolent, if the ending is the same as noted above, then all human activity qualifies as frittering away time. TS 18

If you're not a self-promoter then your life achievements could be thrown down the shitter as a result of not using redundant lame Twitter and understandably then, you will be bitter. TS 18

Truly, Twitter is for people whose lives are already down the shitter. TS 18

Walking around all day long with a smartphone in your hand is a mental illness so don't think that it's not wrong for you to do so you total ding dong! TS 18

After you have almost been killed, what is your utility now? TS 18

Death came to sweep me away even though I didn't believe it could ever happen, yet, I won the victory with the help of Christ and that I will never forget. TS 18

If you cannot even make love to someone, then what the hell do you think you have? TS 18

How fascinating that a once great pontificator has been silenced by death. TS 18

You may have your legacy amongst your generation, but many following generations later - you will be forgotten as if you never even lived. That's a comforting thought in reference to meaningfulness. TS 18

There are too many people overeating because they don't have any vocational leading, and likewise, who can stop such psychological bleeding? TS 18

Right now, someone's dying, someone's getting killed and someone's getting drilled; my, my, my, what a big fish bowl we live in! TS 18

The genius and the artist have one common best friend – the blank page. TS 18

Your past maybe a pisser, but you can overcome it by being and offering the best in the present-tense. TS 18

Some depression is derived of the endocrine system. TS 18

No need for grandstanding just get it done and then go and have some fun. TS 18

What kind of generation doesn't hold the older generation in any kind of worthy esteem? TS 18

We can organize a semblance of functioning social order but our finite memory and intelligence - along with our inability to be present in all geophysical space where social interactions occur - limits how much social order can ever be realized. TS 18

The monastic life is probably an evolved mental illness as well but it does have productive outcomes associated with it. TS 18

Not having an ally in the world is a pretty damn sorry case scenario that's quite depressing and that's not easy confessing, but it certainly needs redressing if that's where you're stressing. TS 18

The person who is completely sane knows the deception of fame and knows chasing it or lusting for it is completely lame and utterly insane. TS 18

Contrary to what people believe, individuals sitting around smoking pot are not lazing around just to rot, but instead, they're thinking great thoughts more than not. TS 18

If I take your access to utilities away from you for a certain amount of time, then I will change you. TS 18

You cannot win them all and some contests just aren't worth the fight; and likewise, the prudent man accepts this as a gospel fact of light. TS 18

Gravity has his will and he is king over humanity. TS 18

Any of the universal laws of physics are attributes of Almighty God's essence and power. TS 18

Honor your agreements and do the right thing to keep strife at bay and secure your home base. TS 18

Spiritual emptiness and no direction is the ultimate price in psychological deflation where you're constantly waiting for its cessation so you can experience life-giving regeneration. TS 18

The world is not looking for Christ and that's its entire problem in a nutshell. TS 18

The adventurous man suffers many inconveniences to go along with his adventures and the suburbanite man envies him; however, the adventurous man does likewise, and wishes he had the consistent comforts and ease of the suburbanite man – so they both live in envy and discontentment. TS 18

When the highlight of your day is being able to get up close to Florita from behind so that she's loving it – then how does a man's day get any better than that? TS 18

Don't be a leader too stupid enough not to call upon your surrounding brain trust or your time in charge will soon be a bust as a result of your lack of trust. TS 18

Life is a short ride where many people have lied, cried and gotten fried – so do yourself a favor and do right so you can ride the blessing tide and don't have to experience the former cited slides (in order to cope) and you'll avoid the slippery slope. TS 18

When you cannot get high and you cannot sleep, it's more than likely that your life has become cheap so what the hell do you think you're going to reap living like a creep? TS 18

If you're blessed enough to fall in love then hopefully it will be with someone who is eligible and ready to freely receive the powerful passionate love you have to give so you can really live. TS 18

Don't confuse relieving your physiological needs and desires with irrational guilt. TS 18

Let's go to Millie's for no frillies! TS 18

Hey asshole, maybe you can look-up from your smartphone now and comprehend that you have no running water to shower or drink with and no electricity to cool your sorry ass down. TS 18

Too bad for those purely good fantasies that never make it to be transformed into a reality. TS 18

Giving love, knowledge and encouragement to people that don't want any of these blessings is as low as it goes and truly utterly blows! TS 18

I'm tired of sitting in shit and watching my life get ripped when I have still remained steady and haven't lost my grip whereas multitudes of others would have went on a self-destructive trip. TS 18

Hate in the heart that doesn't manifest itself in destructive behavior is still better than killing someone. TS 18

What gets you old is not being bold. TS 18

And who can keep their head living the rest of their life in a dead-end? TS 18

Truly, Almighty God doesn't care about your statuses, comfort or material things. If you doubt it, then Christ is your example. TS 18

There really isn't anything that can allay and comfort our death row sentence here upon earth. All the pleasures of life are fleeting and impotent in helping us feel better about what we will inevitably lose when we leave this material world. TS 18

Be strong lest you become a Ding Dong. TS 18

And maybe today is the end of the betrayal that has plagued your entire life in reference to freedom and justice and you will finally obtain access to what is rightfully yours and you will finally smell the Joe, and your life will no longer have to utterly blow. TS 18

Having no propelling goals is a pit of a hole in your soul that will inevitably take its toll and most people surrounding you won't have time to care about your plight or show you any light or encourage you to fight. TS 18

I'm surrounded by hate, apathy, laziness and zero love and I just want it to abate before it's too fucking late! TS 18

There's absolutely nothing coming through to prove a future groove. TS 18

What person is stupid enough to not want a willing mentor in his/her life? Dumber than dumb! TS 18

Ostensibly, there no reward for a job well done so make sure you go out and have a ton of fun so you don't let the former cited bullshit get you undone. TS 18

Depression and hopelessness will make physical pain worse. TS 18

If she's an unrequitor, then simply forget her. TS 18

The bottomless pit is darker than you'll ever want to know and take it from someone that knows a little bit about this oppressive shit. TS 18

What do you know until you're in a place where you're saying, "Lord, if you don't come and heal this bum, I'm going to die numb?" TS 18

When a holy light cannot even heal minds that are blind and uptight, then I would say it's quite a stronghold bind that's left these souls blind from ever comprehending the good associated with being kind along with being able to respond to any outreaching point of shine. TS 18

When you're just living for today and maybe tomorrow, you're more than likely not worrying about the interest and principal on your long-term loan. TS 18

If you don't tell me what's in your heart, then my relationship with you is worth a passing fart and your refusal to part with any of your heart is a dart in my heart. TS 18

Shutting-off your love and saying to others, "Jesus Loves You," is a cruel and misguided notion and set of behavioral actions. TS 18

The courageous man finally gets into his fetal positon to commence his rot in hell. TS 18

Sometimes, getting stoned actually enhances or magnifies your physical pain; therefore, so much for the medical marijuana argument that pot lessens pain. TS 18

And what is a worse feeling than having nowhere to go? TS 18

Our psychological weakness manifests the physical weakness that's already there and exacerbates it. TS 18

The world and its history is primarily about vanity, ignorance, greed, rape, pillage, and murder, and that story is never going to collectively change on any mass scale. TS 18

We celebrate the diversity of cultures but it is the diversity of cultures and our ignorance of them that sets the foundation of distrust amongst people and nations. TS 18

If you're a class (A) asshole then you're not getting any reward from me – regardless of who the hell you delusionally think you are. TS 18

Another day of misery and no miracle and more pain makes Michael less likely to remain sane. TS 18

The spirit of the Anti-Christ has been on the globe for thousands of years and he can do no greater harm than Almighty God allows (see the book of Job) but this current age of apostasy knows no bounds, and likewise, with the advent of chip technology for buying and selling along with smartphone technology for sowing mindlessness – the sedulous devotion to 666 is already here and ready to conquer the cowardly soulless sheeples. TS 18

Youth is fleeting and believing that having a plan will always bring success is extraordinarily misleading and old age is certainly an ass-beating, and likewise, these are undoubtedly life facts that need a heeding. TS 18

Those who are spiritually dead are very unlikely to be led, therefore, trying to reach them before they go to their backyard shed and put a bullet in their head and end-up permanently dead is a very good idea instead! TS 18

Religious glue preached by a few is powerless to motivate those masses that have nothing to do and zero social and intellectual clue. TS 18

What a place to be where you cannot spiritually see and all you can think about regarding life is: Me! Me! Me! TS 18

It's amazing that something that you cannot empirically see is killing you or will slowly kill you regardless of whether you have a clue in reference to what to do. TS 18

The bottomless pit is like being in the shit, and for some, it will cause them to lose their wits. TS 18

The people of long-ago history are the real heroes for they lived their lives without many of the comforts and opportunities we ungratefully enjoy today, yet they still realized productive lives. TS 18

Add something to the social environmental mood by showing a little gratitude rather than your usual shitty attitude that has fomented many a feud because you're such an ignorant dude. TS 18

How many people can stand serenity without jerking-off? TS 18

When it's time to be going – you will be going. TS 18

Having no place to go really blows especially when you're living in place that has never seen snow. TS 18

Shining your light to the lost has a cost and it ain't the bite of Jack Frost or being bossed; however, it's more than likely being socially tossed. TS 18

The geophysical environment that we inhabit is like the lurking phantom. TS 18

A monkey in your wrench might make you pretty tense or if it's chronic, maybe it will make you lose your commonsense or become utterly dense or even physically spent. TS 18

How can you appear psychological secure on Facebook but completely non-secure in your in-person public presentation? Very strange. TS 18

The past is a jewel only rejected by the total fool who fails to discern what a valuable tool it is in order to effectively rule and abandon what is cruel. TS 18

The middle class bondage of a life is rife with spiritual strife and bitching wives. TS 18

Unlock the art within you and see what ensues? TS 18

The bondage of *against your will type of employment* is certainly no enjoyment but it might motivate some souls to join the Unenjoyment line. TS 18

Thank Father God every day for the evolvement of your independent life even though it has been rife with strife and not readily perceptually known to you although nevertheless, you have been amongst the exceptional few. TS 18

Instead of sitting around coping and moping, do some art and get a new start lest you blow too many farts from eating too many Pop Tarts. TS 18

Park your ass in the dark and let's see if you can crawl your ass out to make a stark mark. TS 18

If you've been lucky enough to have felt lust and love simultaneously, then why not go ahead and try to apprehend that jewel again you total fool! TS 18

There's probably at least one diaper buried in every contrived landfill that exists upon earth but it's impossible to know because no one is willing to put the work in to confirm that it's decidedly so! TS 18

Humanity brings out the worst of us in all areas of being human making damn certain no one is ever going to have the acumen and fortitude of Harry S. Truman. TS 18

By the way, the guy that was bragging about his million dollar house just keeled over dead. That investment was ostensibly worth it. TS 18

Life upon Earth: The great dress rehearsal. TS 18

Life is terse and the hearse is in the waiting. TS 18

If you're speaking commonsense in America, then you're speaking Chinese to all native English speakers. TS 18

You cannot take the sexual animal out of a man and thank Almighty God for it or the human race simply could not go on. Lesbians cannot make babies. TS 18

Gracie is someone I wouldn't mind making it to third basee with. TS18

Is it sexual harassment when another guy follows you into the men's room so he can take a piss next to you so maybe he can cop a look at your thingee? TS 18

What's the attraction of attempting to make love to a chick holding a smartphone in her hand? TS 18

So many meaningless lives are playing-out factually or perceptually and the costs are great all across the planet. TS 18

The solution to nation emigration are those 192 nations saying to one particular nation in need, "how can we help you build your nation and what can you do for us in return?" TS 18

There's a lot of people in this world who are where they are geo-physically because they have no place else to go where they won't suffer anymore social economic blows. TS 18

What good is it to hear from Almighty God in your evolved process of serenity if no one is going to listen to you? TS 18

The darkness of life is epitomized by opportunities never birthed that should have been born or opportunities that should have been apprehended but were lost. TS 18

What political capital does a white man married to a Japanese man have living in Japanese society? TS 18

The pleasure of taste never goes to psychological waste and that's why some people have extraordinarily sized waists they need to recreate. TS 18

If you know your intermediate math it should always at least secure the fact that you'll always have a place to take a bath. TS 18

Some people are living in a serious bind because they cannot find someone to be seriously kind. TS 18

And stop to think about all those unfortunate souls who are toiling in the soil and their bodies are always boiling. TS 18

For the astute life is like a game of chess where the ultimate goal is to avoid the social mess, and in the meanwhile, not to become less. TS 18

Destruction outlasts all vanity. TS 18

Constant boredom might ensure the pursuit of some dumb thrills that might actually kill. TS 18

So many people wearing a public self-disguise in order to obscure their lies so as to impress the other guys; however in the long-run scheme of things, this type of lifestyle ain't too wise. TS 18

There's not too many hunks who are deciding that they should become monks and that fact is nowhere close to being defunct or debunked. TS 18

Build your house of brick so you won't have to succumb to any natural disaster's destructive tricks that will make you and your family utterly sick. TS 18

Try to find a first-rate mate so you don't have to commiserate about your sorry fate at a later date. TS 18

The person on a path of woeful waste inevitably will face utter disgrace. TS 18

Hey single guys, maybe you should meet and date a registered nurse who can reverse your life from getting way worse. TS 18

When all of your property is destroyed and it wasn't covered by Lloyd's of London, then it's understandable why you might devolve into a curmudgeon. TS 18

Sometimes, people capitulate their rightful commonsense in order to make their livelihood cents. TS 18

How does the wonderful life lived that has fulfilled a life call end-up on his back staring at a blank ceiling and wall that evokes no emotional response at all? TS 18

For some people, when their life journey is done all they want to do is find a gun so they don't have to suffer a ton because their race has been run and there's no more perceivable fun. TS 18

Higher education in the USA has become a joke that's gone up in smoke and is going broke because excellence cannot be paid. TS 18

You cannot soar living with a whore but she just might become a bore that you'll inevitably have to show the door. TS 18

Mary Jane knows art and the delicious taste of a lightly toasted Pop-Tart. TS 18

What kind of Governor has a mass party for himself to honor his reelection when the land he governs has been laid waste? Total asshole. TS 18

No one mentored my father, and therefore, he didn't mentor me. Lord, send a willing young man to me that I can mentor in order to break this sick curse and set the good energy free. TS 18

The pleasure of desire comes and goes and then it's met and then it's gone. Now doesn't that really blow? TS 18

A Band-Aid over a bleeding aorta or new wine in old wineskins is the instructional way of the imbecile. TS 18

The one thing we never have amnesia about is how the other guy did us wrong. TS 18

Confess what's ever on your chest and relieve yourself from some psychological duress and maybe that beautiful girl will come and give you her life-giving caress that absolutely is the best, and then, you can finally get some rest! TS 18

And how many lonely and confused guys are diligently going to the bar to get drunk because their heads are in a paralyzed funk while in the meanwhile their sex lives have totally shrunk? However, they refuse to become a monk exclaiming, "That's a bunch of bunk that's just for the homosexual punks!" TS 18

Some people have been on a drug for so long that now they need a rug. TS 18

And how many lives are just spinning around like a cyclone with a fateful ending just evaporating out with a moan? TS 18

Your life maybe hanging like some dingleberry dung but be mindful not to get too psychologically stung so that you fall off the life rung. TS 18

Having used *your time wisely* will be your attorney at your final judgment. TS 18

You don't have to apologize for being a spirit encapsulated in a physical body that's hell-bent upon being exhilarated in order to get elevated most of the time. TS 18

The death of getting older is all the laying around making you get astoundingly round. TS 18

Why do you want to look at porno on a smartphone? Instead, why don't you just make it official by going smaller and watch porno under a microscope? Idiots. TS 18

Don't deceive yourself to believe that you can reason with people who have no ability or willingness to reason because they're atavistic rednecks. That's as dumb as dumb is. TS 18

The animal within you relates to the size of the sack and how much love it can pack before it empties itself into total lack to the point where you can never go back. TS 18

Pent-up sexual energy is destroying people's lives today just as it has all throughout history and how can it ever be adequately treated with long-term success? TS 18

Your bitterness probably relates to something that you should do that you won't do. TS 18

Pi's face tries to hide the disgrace but it's obvious that her story is one of debase that needs to be erased in her future days. TS 18

No courage yields empty coffers. TS 18

The affable and itinerant pastor risks adultery every day just for being himself. What a quandary! TS 18

Unfortunately, some people's only hope for salvation is some serious tribulation without cessation until there's comprehension of what needs immediate attention. TS 18

Some older people think a younger presence would kill them but it actually might heal and propel them. TS 18

If your love eviscerates because your lover won't cooperate or negotiate her recalcitrant behavioral actions that just enervates your ability to elevate, then you should probably vacate after you've contemplated that you did all you could to placate. TS 18

If despite the hell that you have lived within you can still contemplate and create first-rate, then you should have the ability to easily self-exonerate. TS 18

Without security, there is no certainty, and under those conditions nothing is going to look too pretty. TS 18

How much pleasure can one pursue and feel without being on a wheel that can never truly reveal the real deal that eventually – everything stops at the end of the reel? TS 18

When you build without pride and you're not on anyone's side, is that not life's best ride? TS 18

If you dined today and you're likewise fully content, then your life is certainly not spent - especially if you can still pay the rent and you're not living in a tent because you make some decent cents, along with the fact that you can talk and teach some commonsense thereby making a social dent without living or thinking hell-bent. TS 18

Why is academia so proud of *referring to someone else* when if left to stand on their own intellectual ground most cannot create knowledge on their own, yet these same jackasses want to be called doctors? Hilarious and pathetic. TS 18

Despite the scorn against it, porn actually works to help the forlorn from getting further torn. TS 18

The global world is utterly immorally far gone because of the prodigious extent of the following behavioral actions:

1. Egocentrism.

2. Greed.

3. Willful ignorance.

4. Jealousy.

5. Hatred.

6. Irrational fear.

7. An inability to communicate.

8. Injustice.

9. Lies.

10. Hedonism, and,

11. No mercy shown to others. TS 18

Show no mercy and get no mercy, and as Ralph exclaimed to Alice, "And you're going to get yours!" TS 18

If you cannot earn in life, then your life will take a serious downturn and until you learn and discern how to earn, you'll be on the burn as the world continues to turn. TS 18

The primal animal in us rules us or attempts to rule us and that's the rule. TS 18

Being successful can make you old too! TS 18

All that daily behavioral activity invested toward just trying to get to the center of that fleeting orgasm experience. TS 18

If you always stay in your fort how are you going to make it to the other port? TS 18

And all those fantasy-based romantic possibilities abscond one by one and now you wish you had a magic wand. TS 18

Mid-life and old age is about making love to yourself most of the time because no one will give you the time of day. TS 18

Truly, contemporary masses of people that surround you will never amount to anything worth a damn in life and you're not to blame for it despite what the liberals erroneously think. TS 18

As a kid, I hated standing in front of stores asking people to donate money for Little League support. One time, I asked this guy if he would like to donate to Little League and he responded, "I doubt it; I doubt it; no, I really doubt it." I then looked and my brother and fellow solicitor and asked, "Do you think he doubts it?" TS 18

Find your *TLC behavioral choices* and cement them into your daily routine – not only for your well-being to be maintained, but as a payback for a lifetime of a job well done! TS 18

Non-reflection time in your life will morph into some form of abuse so make it a priority to underscore the good that has occurred on your behalf and the good that you have done as well so that you can be well. TS 18

It's all sexual inversion energy that's killing most people's mental and physical health. TS 18

An outstanding pretzel stick or hard pretzel will put it all in perspective. TS 18

And how many people are living for something that is not real and they don't want to know the real deal or cannot even hold a conversation with someone during a meal? TS 18

Some people's take is: It's all a heartbreak so what the hell difference does it make? TS 18

Be of good cheer: You could be the hired wedding photographer who ruined every picture taken because your dumb thumb was in them. TS 18

Storybook endings are for story books and many a soul has been took by the fantasy-endings in a book that should never have even been given a serious look. TS 18

The addict meticulously contrives how to maintain his addiction. TS 18

I've had dreams of being close to the railroad tracks with a train coming countless times. What does this mean? TS 18

Housing values have always been unjustifiably inflated. For instance, how does any structure built of worldly materials that erode, truly have any growing equity value? Total bullshit. TS 18

The bondage of our economic lives and the limited amount of trust around us seriously limits what we can do, where we can go, and what we can do to help. TS 18

Not being able to go back is the death of you knowing you. TS 18

The addict knows how to keep his addiction alive through calculated daily planning. TS 18

And oh boy, what is of more joy than watching a young child dance for joy because of getting a toy! TS 18

Harness your meditative state and do some real productive work as a result. TS 18

Zero contemplation keeps Michael on an obtuse path that slowly builds his wrath, and in reference to the simple math, think of what will be the sorry aftermath? TS 18

The man that can make comfort in a den of nails might be someone who should be your pal. TS 18

Great intellect and compassion are two attributes that are rarely found together. TS 18

Why act like you don't want my business because I'm an American? You're the bigot dude for punishing me for what some other sorry American ass dude did that made you come unglued and nurse that tude. TS 18

Unfortunately, it's true that many Filipinos create their own misery. TS 18

The Chinese and the Filipinos can both be very industrious, but the Filipinos don't always work with the best materials. TS 18

What's the Guinness Book of Records for living days without hearing any encouragement? TS 18

Every man needs to hear that encouraging word and don't let his self-assured façade lead you to believe otherwise. TS 18

And think of how many people you could fall in love with, and if all of those options were fulfilled, what kind of life would you be living? TS 18

Water is the best. TS 18

I sit here day after day and no one touches me and no one talks to me and no one knows me. I am like a pristine mountain peak in the Arctic region. TS 18

The sanctity of life is all around you with the precious babies, toddlers and children. See it and live! TS 18

The disabled man with mild cerebral palsy is a courageous daily hero and he certainly has a social life perspective that must be heard. TS 18

And how many total temporary relationships does the modern individual experience in his/her lifetime and what are the psychological ramifications upon his/her life view? TS 18

When we say to a person, "You have a bad witness," what are we really saying? In fact, that person may just be expressing the truth of his genuine heart so would we rather he fake it so we then can concur that he's a good and faithful witness? Total bullshit. TS 18

The church is replete with play-actors who missed their call to the theatre. TS 18

If you can take note of your key instructional points and experiences, then you have the titles and outlines for various books. TS 18

Everyday new decisions have to be made and the manager has to be able to make them accurately – and in doing so – the requisite foundation that accuracy is built upon is physical and intellectual stamina, and only experience can make that foundation a reality. TS 18

Marrying too young has the potential to burn-out the flame of passion quickly. TS 18

The folly of the imaginative mind can know no bounds. TS 18

When your folly becomes a bore, now you're ready to cross over to the *other life shore* and open a new door to realize something way better more. TS 18

Sometimes, the only way the great work gets done is in solitude. TS 18

Stop saying it's all your fault and go and get a malt or a hot soft pretzel covered in salt. TS 18

An American guy I met today in McDonald's was commenting upon the laziness of people going through the drive-thru who didn't want to get out of their cars. He concluded that this was an example of what is wrong with American society. I was amazed that someone even had a passion to give a damn about any surrounding social ills. TS 18

When you don't make an effort to deeply think, the intellectual mind shrinks and your personality really stinks thereby causing you not to get too many winks because you're perceived as a complete dink who cannot even comprehend the beauty and taste of a killer Italian sausage link with a cold glass of Wink. TS 18

Hey chick, stop lying to yourself; your husband doesn't want to come back to live with you because your blubbery ass is too fat and dat's dat! TS 18

Seduction might morph into reproduction or personal or social destruction but rarely reconstruction. TS 18

Marx made a big deal about owning property but he was woefully wrong in reference to making this a life priority in relation to two key instructional facts: 1) No one can truly own the geophysical environment, but rather the geophysical environment owns us, and 2) Being a slave to your own property possessions might cause some grief, loss of freedom of movement and maybe even some lost souls. TS 18

The sardonic man is the man whose aspirations have been unfulfilled – either unjustifiably or willfully. TS 18

The only one who can truly comprehend the incredible life ride you've had is Almighty Father God and tragically because of the world's ignorance and peripatetic pace, most of your story will never be told or known. TS 18

One decision *ye* or *nay* changes life destinies. TS 18

Apprehending the miracles of Almighty God is the testimony of the validity of your salvation. TS 18

If your life legacy known by most is: *all you cared about was yourself* then someone's going to need help with your eulogy. TS 18

The super typhoon is the enema administered. TS 18

How many people have had their place of employment destroyed and they're still working amidst the rubble of it? Is that the shit or what? TS 18

Another day where nobody initiated a conversation with me but I did it at least ten times. TS 18

Why do these chicks pay attention to you when you're with your wife, yet completely ignore you when you're alone? Do they want to have a threesome? TS 18

When it takes you three hours to remember someone's name from the past, you're a frying dude! TS 18

When your movements are not in symmetry with your spirit, it's a sign that something is off in one or more of the other areas of being human. TS 18

The miracle of the miracle is: there are no outside resources available or needed. TS 18

You may need a brain suture to stop worrying about the distant future because really your life experience should underscore the fact that anything can happen at any time, and it might even be something really good! TS 18

Having lunch with the new guy might be the day's point of high, so don't let it pass you by! TS 18

Maybe if you would just preempt a "Hi!" people would stop saying goodbye because you're way too shy. TS 18

The work is all done and I am so grateful and so content, yet I'm sitting in jail now with no further commission to fulfill; however, I am nowhere near being over the hill nor in need of taking any pills, but rather, motivated to carry-out more compelling goodwill. TS 18

Too much personal success can blow-up a marriage quite easily. TS 18

The pleasurable experiences of the social and physical areas of being suffer no everlasting pleasure and must be experienced moment by fleeting moment. Nevertheless, we enjoy the pleasures knowing they will not last; yet even in knowing that pleasures will end, we are thankful for what we have experienced. Unfortunately, we still become consumed with idolatry in our attempt to recreate the pleasures experienced – over and over again. TS 18

I would never tell a little boy not to love heavy equipment or trucks. That would be cruel and unusual punishment. TS 18

Some men cannot get over the fact that there's more to life than chasing beautiful women. TS 18

You're not evolving the human race talking to each other via Walkie Talkies (smartphones). TS 18

Sexual escapades will fry the young man's career. TS 18

The curse of novelty is its short-lived and the varieties that life offers keeps us desiring those diversity of experiences at the expense of previous relationships or pleasures experienced, thereby keeping many lawyers well-fed and making marriages go dead. TS 18

The hell with these bureaucratic regulators who want to dress everyone in the same uniforms and oppress unique behavior and outcomes; such ignorant clowns suck the artistry out of life, and in doing, are not any more efficient in producing effective outcomes because of it. TS 18

Some people fear personal success will destroy their soul hence they avoid it like the plague. TS 18

When old habits actually begin to die, it's time to rise to the sky. TS 18

The location of the idolatry needs a secure ambience to fuel the mood. TS 18

And the darkness wouldn't let the light in ever! And that explains why your plans for excellence and good go for naught most of the time. TS 18

I had the chance to get out of this hellhole while living under optimal circumstances and I didn't get it done and now I'm having a ton of no fun. TS 18

The naysayers motivated by their greedy hearts spew their venom out and your strength of faith and optimism disables their bacterial growth, and consequently, hope and favorable outcomes ensue. TS 18

And what's a greater delusion than self-importance? TS 18

Youth and vanity are two moronic peas in the same pod. TS 18

You're not going to have much good to reap and get a lot of good sleep when you're living too cheap and you're a total creep. TS 18

The bombastic and garrulous fool that has too much to say and thinks he knows the way is the way he is because he's led an ignorant life of never ever having to pay. TS 18

Is Treva done with composing her cover letter yet? I would surely bet it's not done yet. TS 18

People who are the real deal don't need to ever steal and usually have some reliable wheels and some killer daily meals that might even include eating medium-well veal or electric eel. TS 18

The babies in poverty is the world's greatest atrocity. TS 18

The man filled with hope seldom has to cope and he always makes a daily date with the soap. TS 18

Those who fritter away their time ain't worth a dime and their lives go down the shitter and they're the only ones to blame for being bitter. TS 18

And how many people living lies and believing their own bullshit jive are on Facebook live when they're actually living in dives? TS 18

Being a flunk and hanging-out with punks that believe a bunch of bunk will truly get your life sunk. TS 18

Those people who want their lives to remain the same and be placed in a standstill contextual frame are really quite socially and psychologically lame. TS 18

Why don't you stop being a living flop who only can swing a mop when you could open your own shop and find yourself on top? TS 18

There's definitely some morons on the wrong course who are heading for a nasty marriage, relational or work divorce in full force. TS 18

Don't live your life on the fringe because you cannot stop your folly binges thereby completely singeing your opportunities while your family cringes at your willful stupidity. TS 18

If you're at work being successful only because you're a faking, eventually that act will go a tanking and you'll no longer be bringing home the bacon because the truth will be *out-of-the-bag* that your ass was never truly a shaking but only was a taking while you were a faking. TS 18

Finding good people left in this world is like trying to find some still hard robust marshmallows in your near finished bowl of Lucky Charms. TS 18

Nothing is more pathetic than the dying old man that cannot show humility. TS 18

You might be too frail to set your life a sail but before you utterly wail or completely derail, maybe someone or something will arrive in your life to set a fire to your tail before you absolutely fail! TS 18

Those who deceptively beguile take away people's smile, but their long-standing machinations are futile. TS 18

It's all a scam, sham and flim-flam and those who make a lifetime of ingesting Hormel spam will eventually have an arterial jam. TS 18

Let the good times in your life rip at a consistent clip and not be a blip, then your steps will know some zip! TS 18

Some people's mission in life is going fishing or wishing they were always cooking in the kitchen while living in Michigan. TS 18

If you've given-up your vocational search then your life has taken a turn for the worse for being in such a lurch. TS 18

Some people are always proclaiming "mine, mine, mine," but truly they are way out-of-line and in their future time, they will never taste the fine wine. TS 18

The gracious host doesn't mind the gauche guest who rejects most of the main meal for a piece of toast. TS 18

Hopefully in life, you can find a lover who is of sound mind and is very kind and not hell-bent to bind you and allows you ample free time. TS 18

Eventually, those people who are living as fakes will make some huge mistake that someone will not be able to easily take, thereby causing him to jump-off a bridge into the lake. TS 18

Don't be deceived; some people can smoke a lot of pot and still be able to buy a nice lot and have all kinds of opportune shots to raise-up their tots and never socially rot. TS 18

It's true: You can habitually smoke pot and still make it to work on the dot regardless of whether the ignorant naysayers believe it or not. TS 18

The teen that has evolved into a mean sex fiend needs someone to intervene so their potential jail bond doesn't impose an asset lien. TS 18

You can take that Internet and shove-it up your ass! TS 18

Facebook: Another tool for useless egocentric activity and vain blathering's and misguided behavioral actions. TS 18

There are very little difference makers in this life and the talkers and pontificators are not amongst them. TS 18

Don't be in such a haste to take something material and make it into waste because someone just might have a taste for it – so don't deem it shit you total nimwit twit! TS 18

Some people's lives are nothing but hap and it's mostly related to their unconfessed crap and them having no vocational map. TS 18

The ozone's depleting and the curse of life is that all experiences are fleeting. TS 18

Too many unjust and exorbitant life fees will bring people to their knees making it impossible for them ever to see and believe how they can fight back like Bruce Lee? TS 18

Some people are fighters who have lost weight and become lighter and now they inspire people to drink Apple Cedar thereby making their muscles and flabby bodies tighter. TS 18

You may currently be an outcast but get-off the ground and be found and eradicate your past so it doesn't last and you can go forward and astound! TS 18

You better intervene if you have a delinquent teen - especially if he's a sex fiend. TS 18

The old man with no peace will lose his teeth. TS 18

Find your passion or find yourself eating USDA rations. TS 18

If she's wearing the diamond ring band this week and she's highlighted her hair and now she's wearing her hair out, then maybe she either got engaged or she really likes you! TS 18

If she's on stage and her eyes meet yours and you both hold the eye contact for at least 15 seconds, then you will feel her soul and now you'll know. TS 18

The man that cannot cry has already died. TS 18

Some people don't feel comfortable getting nude and lewd and that's why they eat way too much food. TS 18

I don't want to be a don, I just want to tear down deceptive and useless idolatrous icons. TS 18

My day was made when Aileen came running to me to touch my hand and wish me a Merry Christmas. Her gesture was so simply pure and so lovely of an experience deriving from such a purely beautiful human being! TS 18

The world's in total darkness and so little know the way of life and so little who do know the way, have the courage to submit to it and be transformed by it. TS 18

If you care more about the scratches on your car than the girl, then your head needs to be twirled. TS 18

If your motive to serve now is pure, then your salvation is sure because Almighty Father God has transformed you from the sorriness of what you were and that's for blooming sure! TS 18

Don't be saying "I do" because you didn't have a clue when you could have knew. TS 18

If you can pray purely for the welfare of others, then a good work is being faithfully completed in your soul by the Holy Spirit just as promised. TS 18

If your cousin is a millionaire and he never talks to you, then you're definitely not better-off for it. TS 18

If you don't develop an employable craft you might end-up becoming riff raff and be a sorry laugh. TS 18

If she wanted to know your first and last name then she would have asked you - and because she didn't ask you - she doesn't want to know so leave her the hell alone. TS 18

The fairy tale ending is authored in ignorance and it's not only not what you think it is, it's not possible or even good for you anyhow. TS 18

Remember the dead today who are not going to be celebrating Christmas Eve with their families. TS 18

Your options are limited when you're entrapped in your limited routine way of thinking about what is possible for you. So true. TS 18

The girl that is beautiful has to fully comprehend that there are beautiful girls all around her and if she is to stand-out in many other ways, then she must move beyond the tiresome perception of a dime a dozen. TS 18

The crux of many people's immorality is not being willing to go to the cross for the other guy. TS 18

The joy of the child is everything is new. TS 18

Some old people do look seriously burned-out on life. TS 18

The monastic journey that ends in a jail cell is hell but it also does serve as a well in order to tell others about what actually does lead to hell. TS 18

De-dignified geophysical and social environmental living wears out your soul as you try to rise above the filth and cultural excrement. TS 18

You must pay for your privacy, personal space and size and those who can consistently do it in a quality manner are either brilliant, hardworking, blessed or criminal. TS 18

When opportunities are denied over and over again because of evil, the person who has lost because of it could actually give-up. TS 18

Sometimes, your physical oppression is spiritual and that's where you have to apply access to the miracle. TS 18

Some mentally ill persons are physically enabled with great endurance because they are actually demon-powered. True. TS 18

You have to impose an ending dot toward the person who's holding-up your life because he needs to shit or get off the pot before he destroys your lot. TS 18

You cannot blame the man who has habitually suffered for bitching about desiring to know a little victory and elation as pre-empted on his behalf by the pure and goodwill of the other guy. TS 18

Lord, can you mercifully add someone into my life who cares? TS 18

Just for awhile, contemplate the horrible lives led by others and let that fact minister to your soul. TS 18

At least in a meditative environment you can bifurcate the material versus the spiritual world and truly know the difference and function accordingly. TS 18

It's nice to fantasize in order to get a rise, but don't get caught-up in those kind of lies or you might be kissing your stable life goodbye! TS 18

It would be nice to actually get something special directly from those people I am consistently helping. I'm only a human being not God. TS 18

Your near death experience should take care of your thankless attitude problem and that's something to be truly thankful for. TS 18

Island people are a sociological gold mine. TS 18

There's a point in your life where achievements mean nothing to you but that doesn't adversely influence your achievement production. TS 18

Is there something wrong with the girl that cannot stop smiling? TS 18

If you can transcend your sexual appetite you're in another place but I wouldn't expect that to consistently apply to any males aged 15 to 35. Good luck. TS 18

Christie is beautiful: A gorgeous face and a responsible persona, but what's actually really motivating her to be responsible as her life goals still seem aimless? TS 18

So many people will never experience the material glory of the United States. TS 18

The girl has a gorgeous caboose that would set a fire in any man loose and might even impair his ability to deduce or produce for a time being. TS 18

To be enamored by the beauty of a woman and her likewise on your behalf – it doesn't get any better than that regarding life's best offerings. TS 18

Men, when your life work is done, you could be and rightfully should be called one of God's sons. TS 18

Don't stand around and do what your friends do; get-off the loo and wear another shoe and realize something new and maybe even be a leader too! TS 18

If someone wants to know you they'll make the effort, and if they don't want to know you, they won't make the effort so chill and don't impose your will. TS 18

Death doesn't care about your life achievements or who will be experiencing bereavement when you're gone. TS 18

What do you think you know until you've had the roof blown-off your house and you had to scurry-away like a scared little house mouse? TS 18

If you have achieved greatness, it's certainly ok if it was somewhat delayed in lateness. TS 18

Invest your time making beautiful rhymes and maybe someday, someone will come into your life who's a great find because she's awfully kind, and then, maybe you won't be in such a spiritual bind. TS 18

A fool might lust after his jewels but if he bumps his head on the bottom of his swimming pool his persona might not ever again be cool. TS 18

Your internal inferno for something you really believe in and passionately love should be a part of your eternal life blessing from Almighty Father God. It will likely be so. TS 18

Infatuation unrequited becomes an incarceration for *the loser in this life* draining dyadic relationship. TS 18

We have a tendency to segregate from the congregate those who refuse to regenerate and do so out of our ignorant bigoted hate. TS 18

If your life has been great, expect a lot of hate deriving from those who do not nor ever will have what it takes to rate. TS 18

Those in leadership who cannot negotiate or collaborate will help eviscerate the state or will obstruct the movement of freight by serving as visionary dead-weight. TS 18

The spirit-created man in a physical body living in a geophysical material world that he cannot fully control is the foundation of all of his problems regardless of how he feels about it. TS 18

Chronic physical pain can eradicate temporarily anything meaningful to you. TS 18

We all have our morphine candy – whether it's food, porn, spending money, aggrandizement, drugs, inane risk-taking, sexual conquest, etc. TS 18

Achieving a level of excellence in any area of life is usually a pretty lonely place to be. TS 18

When the old man doesn't even have it in him to wish you a Merry Christmas or a Happy New Year, you know his physical impairments are wasting him away now. TS 18

Most of us are more far gone than we ever can fully perceptually know. TS 18

The miracle of the physical body of flesh is that it takes so much abuse, yet it does not come loose or go obtuse; and if that is factually correct – then it's explained by the mercy and grace of Almighty God. TS 18

The white flag regarding anomie's destruction of intimacy is the texting revolution. TS 18

What do you think you know until you've been the dying man on the side of the road in the Good Samaritan story? TS 18

Your calling in life might just be that you're a stalwart figure of moral consistency while living amidst the blight, and therefore, you're the only light that shines bright regarding what is right! TS 18

When the body's dying, it has its own will toward finalizing the kill. TS 18

If you're alone, it's most likely because people don't believe what you believe and don't care to believe what you believe. TS 18

The power of humidity's debilitating impact upon the body is that it can even make your teeth hurt. Wild. TS 18

The visionary and effective administrator is dead in the water without capital. TS 18

If all the Board of Directors care about is functioning in status quo, then they all should be given the heave-ho. TS 18

A Godless way to go, is to die alone. TS 18

The challenge for the young man mired in poverty is to actually believe that he can become something else. TS 18

Daily miracles abound and astound, but willful ignorance does not allow them to help people be found prior to their having a permanent date with going underground. TS 18

And try to get your fill of those people that pre-empt goodwill without the use of any monetary bills. TS 18

It's nice to look at beauty, but if you're lusting after what you cannot have, then that will get you pretty moody. TS 18

Some people's living malaise and its adverse impact upon them is like bad mayonnaise and that part of their lives needs to be tased. TS 18

If you park your life in the dark, you might not ever make any laudable stark legacy mark. TS 18

Some people revel in being called 'Doc" when what they truly don't know might be a shock worthy to be mocked. TS 18

The man who mumbles may socially stumble or even crumble, along with the fact that he most likely will not be leading the rumble. TS 18

Petition Almighty Father God for a mission instead of sitting around wishing or choosing to go fishing. TS 18

You don't have to be tall to play basketball but if you idolize going to the mall maybe that passion is obscuring your true call? TS 18

The governing or managing man that cannot hear, contributes to what is behaviorally austere; however, when he's canned, no one sheds a tear. TS 18

The man who perennially sits upon his duff doesn't have it too rough, yet he most likely will not be realizing anything great soon enough as a result of always stuffing his face with Coco Puffs. TS 18

If you sit down and have an audience with someone who is dying, then maybe you'll comprehend that your life of habitually lying will not have people crying when they find out you're dying. TS 18

If you make a date to become great, maybe you'll actually realize a better fate along with the best help mate who's persona does not hold one iota of hate. TS 18

Why would Almighty God allow a cataclysmic disaster to destroy someone's 35-year-old Bible? TS 18

CPSIA information can be obtained
at www.ICGtesting.com
Printed in the USA
BVHW030838240419
546160BV00034B/157/P